Henry Owen

The Intent and Propriety of the Scripture Miracles Considered and Explained

In a Series of Sermons, Preached in the Parish Church of St. Mary Le-Bow, in the

Years 1769, 1770, and 1771 - Vol. 1

Henry Owen

The Intent and Propriety of the Scripture Miracles Considered and Explained
In a Series of Sermons, Preached in the Parish Church of St. Mary Le-Bow, in the Years 1769,
1770, and 1771 - Vol. 1

ISBN/EAN: 9783337159832

Printed in Europe, USA, Canada, Australia, Japan

Cover: Foto ©Lupo / pixelio.de

More available books at **www.hansebooks.com**

THE

INTENT AND PROPRIETY

OF THE

SCRIPTURE MIRACLES

CONSIDERED AND EXPLAINED,

In a SERIES of

SERMONS,

Preached in the Parifh Church of

St. MARY LE-BOW,

In the Years 1769, 1770, and 1771;

For the LECTURE founded by

The Hon. ROBERT BOYLE, Efq;

By the Rev. Dr. HENRY OWEN,

Rector of St. OLAVE, Hart-Street.

And FELLOW of the ROYAL SOCIETY.

IN TWO VOLUMES.

VOL. I.

LONDON,

Printed by *W. Bowyer* and *J. Nichols:*

For J. and F. RIVINGTON, in St. Paul's Church-Yard.

MDCCLXXIII.

TO

THE MOST REVEREND FATHERS IN GOD,

FREDERICK,

LORD ARCHBISHOP OF CANTERBURY;

ROBERT,

LORD ARCHBISHOP OF YORK:

TO THE RIGHT HONOURABLE

LORD GEORGE CAVENDISH,

LORD FREDERICK CAVENDISH, AND

LORD JOHN CAVENDISH,

TRUSTEES FOR THE LECTURE FOUNDED BY

THE HONOURABLE ROBERT BOYLE, ESQ.

THESE SERMONS,

PREACHED BY THEIR APPOINTMENT,

ARE, WITH ALL GRATITUDE

AND HUMILITY, INSCRIBED BY

THE AUTHOR.

PREFACE.

A Short fketch of what is now contained in the following Difcourfes was drawn out, and exhibited to the public in a fmall tract, fo long ago as the year 1755. As I heard of no objectious made to the principles of that treatife, I thought it advifeable, when appointed Preacher of Mr. Boyle's Lecture, to profecute the plan laid down therein, and to extend it to its full dimenfions. And this I determined the rather to do, as fo little had been written on the fubject of *miracles*, by any of my predeceffors in the fame office.

The

The *general* doctrine of *miracles* having been so fully stated by several authors of great note, I had no occasion to dwell much upon it. If I have been successful in applying it to *particular* cases; and consequently in explaining some of the most extraordinary, and therefore the most disputable, parts of Scripture; my design is completely answered—and my appointment, I trust, not wholly unfulfilled.

Whatever observations my reading or meditation could supply on the subject, these I have endeavoured to bring all together into one regular and consistent scheme: the parts of which harmoniously conspire, not only to support and illustrate each other, but also to form a *grand whole*—manifestly expressive of the wisdom and goodness of divine Providence, and clearly demonstrative of the truth and certainty of our holy religion.

In the construction and conduct of this scheme, I had, I must own, a particular

view

view to the benefit and improvement of young Divines; for whofe ufe I have in-ferted fome quotations, which are to be looked upon, not fo much in the light of *proofs*, as of *references* to the authors who have difcuffed the points more at large. The fcheme itfelf will, however, afford them a general *key* to the whole Scripture; as it will fhew them the *grounds* of the feveral difpenfations, and point out the *reafons* why each of them proceeded in the manner it is obferved to do.

They will here fee a grand defign planned from the beginning—they will fee this de-fign carried on by various means, and in va-rious forms, through the feveral periods of the world—they will fee the propriety of thefe forms and methods, in their adapta-tion to the ftate and circumftances of the time in which they took place—they will fee them all working together, and at laft uniting in the perfect accomplifhment of the end propofed; the redemption and recovery

A 4 of

of fallen man —they will therefore, of courfe, fee revelation in its proper light ; and be the more convinced of its reafonablenefs, truth, and divinity,

For a more particular information of the true fcope and intent of the work, it may be of ufe to obferve, that it naturally divides itfelf into *fix* parts.

Part the *firft*, comprehended in Sermon I—III. treats of " the analogy of revealed religion with the conftitution and courfe of nature—and of the credibility and certainty of miraculous interpofitions."

Part the *fecond*, comprehended in Sermon IV—VI. treats of " the moral ftate of the world from the creation to the deluge ; the nature of the difpenfations relative thereto ; and the propriety of the miracles interwoven with them."

Part the *third*, comprehended in Sermon VII—X. treats of " the moral ftate of

the

the world from the deluge to the departure out of Egypt; the feveral difpenfations relative thereto; and the miraculous interpofitions by which they were fupported."

Part the *fourth*, comprehended in Sermon XI—XVI. treats of " the moral ftate of the world from the departure out of Egypt to the end of the Babylonifh captivity; the feveral difpenfations relative thereto; and the fuitablenefs of the miracles, which occur in that period, to the great end they were defigned to promote." . .

Part the *fifth*, comprehended in Sermon XVII. treats of " the moral ftate of the world at the time of our Saviour's appearance—and of the neceffity of a new revelation."

Part the *fixth*, comprehended in Sermon XVIII—XXIII. treats of " the connection between the doctrines of Chrift and the moral exigences of mankind—and of the analogy between his miracles and doctrines."

Conclufion—Sermon XXIV.

More

More errours have escaped me in super-vising the press, than I could wish. Those which particularly affect the sense, and which are marked with an *asterisk*, the Reader is desired to correct in the following manner:

VOL. I.

P.	L.		P.	L.	
6	17	* that the scriptural	109	N. 5.	version
38	20	breathe	149	3.	dele that
64	10	* and how will you	165	Note (ᶜ)	Aſhur
78	13	* of his condition	239	N. 6.	prodiderunt
86	19	* once failed him,	Ibid.	ult.	τηλαυγὶς'
99	8	paradiſiacal	266	Note (ᵐ)	4 florem
Ibid.	13	conſciences	267	18	* was it.

CON-

CONTENTS

OF

VOLUME I.

SER-

committed, and of all their hard speeches which ungodly sinners have spoken against him."

S E R M O N   VI.

GEN. vi. 3.

And the Lord said, My spirit shall not always strive with man; for that he also is flesh: yet his days shall be an hundred and twenty years.

S E R M O N   VII.

GEN. xi. ver. 4—8.

And they said, Go to, let us build us a city, and a tower, whose top may reach unto heaven; and let us make us a name, lest we be scattered abroad upon the face of the whole earth.

And the Lord came down to see the city and the tower, which the children of men builded.

And the Lord said, Behold, the people is one, and they have all one language; and this they begin to do: and now nothing will be restrained from them, which they have imagined to do.

Go

S E R M O N IX.

Jude, ver. 7.

S E R M O N X.

Psalm lxxviii. 12.

S E R M O N XI.

Deut. xxxii. 9, 10.

SER-

S E R M O N   XII.

Psalm xliv. 3.

S E R-

SERMON I.

1 PET. iii. 15.

Be ready always to give an anſwer to every man, that aſketh you a reaſon of the hope that is in you, with meekneſs and reverence.

IT is the plain intention of the Apoſtle in the text, to exhort Chriſtians of every degree, to furniſh themſelves with ſuch a competent knowledge of the principles and evidences of the religion they profeſs, as to be always ready, always prepared, to ſtand up in its defence and ſupport; and to render, whenever they are called upon, a clear, juſt, and ſatisfactory account of it : ſuch an account as may convince any candid, unprejudiced inquirer, that their " faith and

VOL. I.   B   hope"

hope ᵃ " are well grounded; have a folid foundation in truth and reafon; and confequently, that they act a moft rational part in believing and profeffing that religion, which conveys to them fuch affured hopes.

But though the exhortation is addreffed to Chriftians in general, and requires no more than what Chriftians in general are able to perform; for the evidences of religion, and its leading principles, are in the main obvious to the moft common underftanding: yet it muft be owned, that feveral objections have been made to both; both to the proofs, and to the principles of religion; which require for their folution a much larger ftock of learning and knowledge, than falls to the fhare of its ordinary profeffors; and which therefore might be apt to weaken at leaft, if not to " overthrow the faith of fome ᵇ," were they left, unaffifted, to defend themfelves.

ᵃ So read fome ancient Latin copies, and the Syriac verfion. Comp. ch. i. 21.
ᵇ 2 Tim. ii. 18.

Knowing

Knowing then the artifices and fophiftry of unbelievers, who conftantly " lie in wait to deceive [c] "; and fenfible of the benefit, the very great benefit, of guarding the more ignorant, but well-meaning Chriftian from their infidious affaults; it became the concern of the pious Founder of this LECTURE, who nobly defended religion by his writings, and eminently adorned it by his life; it became, I fay, his concern, efpecially when he faw the bold and threatning encroachments of infidelity, to ftrengthen the hands of believers againft it, and to fupply them with proper arms of defence.

With this view, and in a manner the moft likely to accomplifh the end, he exprefly provided by his laft Will and Teftament, that a fucceffion of Preachers might be continued on, whofe province it fhould be to clear and explain the fundamentals of religion; to collect and illuftrate the evidences of it; to remove the objections, which from time to time might be urged againft it; and thereby to inftruct and enable

[c] Ephef. iv. 14.

B 2   their

their hearers to give an anfwer to all, who might prefs them with doubts and queftions about it.

At my entrance then on the duties of this office, and by way of introduction to the principal defign which I have propofed to myfelf in the execution of it; I think it neceffary to befpeak your attention to a certain point or *poftulatum*, that lies at the bottom both of the Philofopher's inftitution, and the Apoftle's exhortation.

And the point is this—

" That our religion is capable of a rational defence"—or elfe it had been to little purpofe, either for the one to require us, or for the other to appoint us, to give a reafon for it.

But it is indeed from this principle, from the confcioufnefs, if I may fo fpeak, of its own rationality, that our religion difdains to be taken upon truft; that it urges itfelf to a trial; and defires no other favour, but that of a fober and difpaffionate examination: fure then of approving itfelf, to the conviction of any candid inquirer, as a wife and

gracious

gracious inftitution; highly conducive to the real happinefs of mankind; and exhibiting, in the form of its feveral difpenfations, evident marks of its divine original.

To a cool, candid reafoner it muft appear, I think, fomewhat ftrange, that the Deift, who is fo ready to acknowledge this *material* fyftem, which we now behold, to be the real workmanfhip of God, fhould yet be fo averfe from admitting the truth, and owning the divinity of that *fpiritual* fyftem, which ftands revealed in the holy Scriptures. For, if the frame of the world fpeaks God for its author; if the attributes of the Deity are plainly difcernible from the works of creation; if the ftupendous grandeur and aftonifhing immenfity of the whole fabric point out his fupreme *power*; if the beautiful fymmetry, regular difpofition, and admirable propriety of the feveral parts, are manifeft indications of his infinite *wifdom*; if the harmonious tendency and concurrence of all, towards the fupport and welfare of the fyftem, proclaim the excellency of his *goodnefs*: if thefe manifeftations in the *ma-*

terial

terial world refer us up to God, and prove
that his hand produced, and directs it; muſt
not the like manifeſtations in the *ſpiritual*
world neceſſarily refer us to the ſame perfect
Being?

Now, if we look into the Scriptures,
where that world is repreſented to us, we
ſhall clearly perceive, if we are not blinded
by ſome inveterate prejudice, the very ſame
ſignatures of divinity—equal exertions of
power, analogous diſpoſitions of *wiſdom*, and
ſimilar intentions of *goodneſs*—impreſſed on
the works of grace, as are manifeſted in
the works of nature. And therefore, if we
judge of *moral*, as of *natural* things, we muſt
needs allow, ſince the *criteria* are of the ſame
kind, that that *ſcriptural* ſyſtem of religion
was at firſt planned, and all along ſupported, by the ſame great and gracious
Being, who created and governs the *natural*
ſyſtem of the world.

If nature be eſteemed " the power of
God, and the wiſdom of God," operating
to the welfare of the body; religion is as
evidently " the power of God, and the wiſdom

dom of God [d]," operating to the salvation of
the soul. To be convinced of this, we need
only attend to the striking analogy, that
subsists between them.

If we see, as we cannot but see, that the
constitution and course of nature is wisely
accommodated to the security and welfare of
the *animal* life [e] ; and that this accommoda-
tion is applied and continued, not by one
uniform immutable process, but by a course
of agency variously diversified, according to
the various relations of the creatures, and
the various necessities to which they are subject: do we not also see, that the scheme
of religion, or the œconomy of grace, is
adapted in like manner to the security and
happiness of the *spiritual* life ; and that, to
answer this purpose, the administration of
the Deity is variously diversified, according
to the various states and conditions, or the
moral exigences, of mankind?

[d] 1 Cor. i. 24.

[e] Incolumitatis ac salutis omnium causa videmus hunc statum
esse hujus totius mundi atque naturæ. Cicero de Orat.
Lib. iii. § 45.

If

If we fay that Providence originally fubjected the *natural* world to the direction of
certain laws, calculated to fupport and maintain its conftitution; does not the Scripture
fay, that he alfo placed the *moral* world
under the like regulation?

If we find, that, when natural bodies
begin to be impaired, a certain principle
takes place, in order to fupply the wafte, and
reftore them to their priftine condition;
do we not alfo find, that revelation comes
in with the like defign, to repair the
breaches of morality, and to reinftate mankind in their original uprightnefs?

In fine, If we perceive that the order and
difpofition of nature tends to promote the
very fame end, that revelation is defigned to
accomplifh; if both of them operate, in
their refpective ways, to the advancement
of virtue, and the fuppreffion of vice; what
elfe can we conclude, but that both are
parts of one moral fyftem, and make up
together cue regular fcheme of providence
for the general happinefs of mankind *

ᶠ See Bp. BUTLER's Analogy, part II. chap. 3.

For

For fince the natural and the revealed difpenfation of things do thus mutually accord,
thus clofely unite, and co-operate with each
other; the plain confequence is, that both
are derived from the fame caufe and author.
But God is univerfally acknowledged to be
the author of nature: and He muft therefore, on the fame principles, be acknowledged
the author of revelation too.

And if revelation comes from this perfect
Being, the fountain of all wifdom and goodnefs; we are hence furnifhed with a ftrong
argument *à priori*, that the whole fyftem of
it, and its feveral parts, muft be founded on
the higheft *reafon*. For infinite wifdom will
always act conformably to itfelf in all its difpenfations.

Accordingly, if we defcend lower — try
and examine the contents of revelation; and
argue the point *à pofteriori*, from its *internal*
character; the reafonablenefs and importance,
the truth and divinity of it will inftantly appear in a full and confpicuous light. The
excellency of its doctrines, the purity of its
precepts, the propriety of its inftitutions,
and the weight of its fanctions, all confpire

to

to fix and afcertain the defcent it claims;
and to prove it as truly worthy of God, as
it is ufeful and beneficial to mankind.

If we proceed on to its *external* proofs ; to
the feveral atteftations that have been made
to it: if we confider the prophecies that
have been fulfilled, and the miracles that
have been wrought, in confirmation of it:
prophecies, which none but he alone, whofe
knowledge is infinite, could poffibly dictate;
and miracles, which exhibit the cleareft indication of the finger of God: " works,
fuch as none could do, except God were
with him [g]:" if we ferioufly attend to thefe
amazing exertions of knowledge and power,
which have been repeatedly, and in the
moft public manner, difplayed in fupport of
the feveral portions of this grand fyftem of
Scripture revelation : if we confider properly
their nature and end; and eftimate the
weight they carry with them ; we fhall find
them fufficient, in all reafon, to evince the
truth of thofe difpenfations, of which they
make fo remarkable a part.

[g] John iii. 2.

Indeed,

Indeed, the fufficiency of them for this purpofe is in fact evident. For numbers of people, in different ages and countries, actually embraced the particular revelations delivered to them, as true and divine, on the ftrength and authority of that evidence, which thefe exertions fupplied. And though the fplendor of the light, which revelation ·diffufed ; and the awfulnefs of the miracles, that were performed in confirmation of it; might render this evidence more fenfibly affecting to thofe, who were eye and ear-witneffes, than it can be to us, who receive it through the medium of hiftorical information : yet is there ftill ftrength enough, ftill weight and force enough in it, to fatisfy any capable and fair reafoner, of the truth of the religion, it is brought to atteft. Nay, upon the whole, WE ftand now, in this refpect, on full as good, if not, perhaps, on better ground, than the moft advantageous of our predeceffors.

The *intrinfic* excellency of revealed religion; the noblenefs of the end it propofes; and the propriety of the means, by which that

that end is profecuted: *thefe* characters of its divinity are full as clear and apparent to us, as ever they were to the acuteft of thofe who lived in the ages before us.

And with regard to its *external* proofs: they are fo admirably conftructed in their nature, and have been fo fecurely guarded in their conveyance downwards, that they ftill fhine forth, and ftrike the mind with equal force and luftre. And if one branch of them be now diminifhed, the other is proportionably increafed: if miracles are ceafed, prophecies are daily accomplifhed; fo that the balance is ftill kept even; and the fum total of the evidence muft appear nearly the fame to us, as it did to our re-moter anceftors. If there be any difference, it lies plainly on our fide. For, as we are favoured with a more extenfive view of this wonderful fyftem, fo we can more clearly fee the dependencies and connections of its feveral parts; their united tendencies to one grand defign; and the furprifing progrefs that is already made towards the actual com-pletion of it.

And

And when we fee, in the courfe of this progrefs, fuch a number of prophecies and miracles, running down through the long extent of five thoufand years; all of them working together; all of them uniting their forces; and forming a chain of connected facts, every link of which communicates ftrength to every other :—When we fee this to be the cafe; the evidence refulting from fuch a combination, manifeftly proves the whole plan to be infinitely fuperior to any *human* contrivance. That wifdom, which could guide a progreffion of facts, through fo immenfe a tract of time, with an uniform direction to one determinate end, could certainly be no other, than the wifdom that forefees all future events: and that power, which could guard it through all the interruptions of the greateft revolutions, and and all the embarrafments of the moft untoward occurrences, could certainly be no other, than the power which governs the affairs of the world [h]. In fo effectual a man-

[h] ROTHERAM's Sketch of the one great argument. §. VII. P. 55.

ner

ner does the general harmony, that runs
through the fyſtem of revealed religion, ſet
forth the truth and divinity of it; and, at
the ſame time, aſcertain the *reality* of the
prophecies and miracles; which are ſo intimately connected; and interwoven with it.

And as to the *proofs*, which theſe prophecies and miracles ſupply, in their turn, for
the ſupport and confirmation of the ſyſtem;
we have no reaſon to ſuſpect, as I ſaid before, that they are in the leaſt weakened, or
diminiſhed in their force, becauſe we ſtand
at ſuch a diſtance from them. For if they,
who were co-eval with the miracles or prophecies, had the evidence of their ſenſes for
the truth of thoſe particular facts that fell
under their notice; we are poſſeſſed of this
ſuperior advantage, that we have all the facts
in view at once; can ſee and contemplate the
whole ſeries entire; and can deliberately examine its ſtrength and connection, throughout
all its parts. What they ſaw, piece by piece,
in a diſjointed manner, we ſee connected and
combined together; built up into a regular,
ſolid and beautiful ſtructure; and from the
excel-

excellency of the work can clearly difcover the wifdom and abilities of its divine Architect.

So far we advance on the credit of Scripture, confidered only as an hiftorical narration of facts. But we are farther to obferve, that God has not left us to mere hiftorical information for the reality and exiftence of thofe prophecies and miracles, on which we ground our belief. There is one monument now ftanding before our eyes, confifting both of prophecy and miracle—I mean the prefent ftate of the Jews—which bears teftimony to the truth of revelation, in an ample, vifible manner; and will probably continue to bear teftimony to it, till it has effectually triumphed over the infidelity of the Gentile, and the obftinacy of the Jew; till it has brought down the proud, exalted notions of the one, and the fallacious, fophiftical reafonings of the other, into an humble and willing obedience to the faith of Chrift. And then, both parties, both Jews and Gentiles, will fee with admiration, that " the weapons of our warfare"—the arguments arifing

I
from

from prophecies and miracles—" are mighty through God to the pulling down of ftrong holds [1] ; " to the fubduing of the prejudices, and clearing of the difficulties, that ftand in the way of Faith.

Such reafons have we to believe, that the Scripture-revelation is derived from God: and equal reafons have we to hope, that it will finally lead us, if we obey its dictates, to a ftate of perfection and happinefs. If we fteadily adhere to thefe reafons, which unite and confirm the whole of revelation; we fhall never be moved by thofe minute objections, which are chiefly drawn from the fancied blemifhes, or falfe reprefentation of *detached* parts. Revelation is a fyftem; and it is to no purpofe to attempt the fub-verfion of it by the demolition of particular portions. For the connection that runs through the whole, cements it fo firmly to-gether, that it muft either ftand or fall in one entire body. But no man has been yet hardy enough to attack it in this compacted form. And if thofe forward critics, who

[1] 2 Cor. x. 4.

talk

talk with fo much petulance and boldnefs
of the defects or deformities of particular
parts, could be prevailed upon to view them
in their relation to the general fyftem, they
would foon alter their opinion of them;
and from being, what they now are, the
fubject of their ridicule, they would become
the object of their admiration and regard.

From fuch an extended and comprehenfive
view, it would manifeftly appear, that all
thefe imagined irregularities, all thefe fcem-
ing defects or deformities, detract no more
from the *beauty* of revelation, than craggy
mountains and fhelving vallies detract from
the *rotundity* of the globe.　Nay, it would
appear, upon clofer examination, that the
former in the *moral*, as the *latter* in the *natural* world, are of great ufe and fervice;
perhaps indifpenfably neceffary to the benefit
and perfection of the whole.　For then it
would appear, that fome of them contain
vaft, latent *mines* of wifdom and goodnefs;
whilft others ferve to convey down to more
diftant places the *furplus* of thofe bleffings,

VOL. I.　　　　　C　　　　　which

which copioufly fell on fome particular
fpots.

But, notwithftanding thefe fair and rational deductions, men of perverfe minds will
ftill cavil and find faults; will ftill raife
new objections, as faft as the *old* ones are
cleared off. And hence it is, that the Apoftle
is fo earneft with us, to " be *always* ready
to give a reafon of the hope, or faith, that
is in us :"—as well knowing, that, in every
age of the church, fuch a preparation would
be highly neceffary : fince in every age, op-
ponents to religion would perpetually arife,
who fhould call forth its profeffors to the
perpetual exercife of their zeal and knowledge. And perhaps, had it not been for
the oppofition of fuch adverfaries to roufe
them, its profeffors might have gradually
funk into a deplorable ignorance of the *doc-*
trines of religion, as well as into a fhameful
neglect of the *duties* of it. This however is
certain, that the cavils raifed againft religion
have all along providentially ferved to promote its intereft. For they have excited a
noble fpirit of inquiry : in confequence of
which,

which, the Scriptures came to be every day more diligently ftudied, more clofely examined, and more critically canvaffed, than, in all probability, they would otherwife have been. And the refult is, that the grounds of our faith are now much better, and more generally underftood; and the objections againft them are of courfe more eafily anfwered [k]. And here let it be remarked, that a difficulty in religion, or an objection to it, once removed, becomes afterwards equivalent to a *pofitive* argument in its favour: adapted to refrefh the faith of believers; and to keep them more ftedfaft and fixed in their profeffion.

Confiderations thefe, that fhould make us attentive to the *latter* part of the Apoftle's advice; and treat our adverfaries "with meeknefs and reverence." For, with regard to *us*, all their attempts have turned out to our fignal advantage [l]; which fhould therefore extinguifh our refentment againft them.

[k] See GERARD's Differtations on the *Genius* and *Evidences* of Chriftianity. Differt. II. § 3.

[l] GERARD, Diff. II. § 4.

And,

And, with regard to *them*, the only way to
work their converfion is to apply to their
reafon with civility and refpect. Illiberal and
violent methods of defence are prejudicial to
any caufe : they render the *beft* fufpicious. It
is our boaft, that our religion is founded
on argument : let it therefore be our bufinefs
to defend it by argument. But every argument, to maintain its force, fhould be propofed in the fpirit of candor and benevolence. If bitternefs and arrogance be mixed
with it, it will lofe of its weight in proportion as men are difgufted at the rudenefs
with which it is offered. Whereas, had it
been ftated in a milder way, it might happily have operated with its whole influence,
to the comfort of the propofer, and the conviction of the adverfary.

And this method is the more to be regard-
ed, becaufe it was the method purfued by
the Apoftles : who, though they fcorned to
enflate the world by " the enticing words
of man's wifdom[m]," were yet careful to convey their arguments in a mild and perfuafive

[m] 1 Cor. ii. 4.

manner-

manner—" in meeknefs inftructing thofe
that oppofed themfelves," as the moft likely
means of bringing them over " to the
acknowledgment of the truth[n]." They
fubmitted the proofs and evidences of their
religion to a free and impartial examination;
and then left them to operate on the minds
of their hearers, according to their weight
and ftrength. And what was the confequence? Why, by thefe means, Chriftianity
made a quick and furprifing progrefs; fpread
itfelf with amazing rapidity over all the
moft celebrated, all the moft enlightened;
kingdoms of the world; filencing the oppo-
fitions of vain philofophy, and triumphing
over the power of civil policy; and, what
were ftill harder to be conquered, over the
prejudices and paffions of mankind. But the
fame evidence, and the fame efficacy it had
at firft, our religion ftill retains. It was
brought to the teft in every age; and in
every age has ftood the trial. Nay, the
more it has been tried, the brighter it has
appeared; and when fairly reprefented, has

[n] 2 Tim. ii. 25.

been

been too piercing and amiable to fail of its juft effect.

It had one advantage, indeed, in the beginning, which the corruption of later times has unhappily deprived it of: I mean, the advantage of appearing in its native drefs, and adorned " with the fruits of good living." This appearance gained on the affections of mankind, and charmed the world into an admiration of it. For, who of any ingenuity of mind, could help admiring a religion, that fhone forth with fo much amiablenefs; and exhibited in its effects fuch a fulnefs of " grace and truth !"

Now, in order to replace it on its proper bafis, and reftore it to its ancient honours, let us bring it again to the ftandard of Scripture ; and endeavour by our lives, as well as by our arguments, to illuftrate the power of it. The end of faith is virtue : and if our life be accordingly anfwerable to our faith, its evidence will be almoft irrefiftible. The divine excellency of it will appear confpicuous in the purity of converfation it infpires; and the divine authority of it will

be

be clearly feen in the goodly fruits it produces. By thus fulfilling the true defign of
our own faith, we may recover others to the
acknowledgment of it. For to make " our
light fo fhine before men, that they may fee
our good works," is, perhaps, one of the
ftrongeft inducements we can fet before
them to imitate our example; to engage
them to embrace the fame faith; and by the
practice of the fame virtues, " to glorify our
Father, who is in heaven⁰." To whom,
with the Son and the Holy Ghoft be afcribed all honour and glory, &c. *Amen.*

⁰ Matth. v. 16.

SERMON II.

1 PET. iii. 15.

*Be ready always to give an answer to every
man, that asketh you a reason of the hope that
is in you.*

IT is surprising to observe, says an inge-
nious writer [p], how closely the most in-
teresting and momentous truths are connected together; and in how regular a train
they issue forth, and flow from each other.

That there is a God, the frame of the
universe, on every part of which the signa-
tures of divinity are so visibly impressed,
plainly demonstrates to us.

But if there be a God, the creator and
governor of the world; then there must be,

---

[p] SEED, vol. II. Serm. VI.

of

of courfe, fome homage due to him from
his rational and dependant creatures : that is,
in other words, there muft be fome religion.
And if fome religion be neceffary, it muft
be fuch a religion as is properly calculated
for the general benefit of mankind. And
what religion is there in the world, that is
fo well adapted to the circumftances, and
makes fo noble a provifion for the improvement and happinefs of mankind, as that
which is revealed in the holy Scriptures?

Such reflections as thefe naturally remind
us of the precept in the text, and prepare
us in fome meafure for the difcharge of it.
They lead us to examine the grounds of our
religion, and to weigh the evidences by
which it is fupported. Thefe refearches into
the grounds and evidences of it, will enable
us, according to the degrees of our proficiency, to " give an anfwer to every man,
that afketh us a reafon of the hope that is
in us."

But to render ourfelves fuch mafters of
the fubject, as to be able to return a fatisfactory anfwer, and to fhew the reafonable-

nefs

nefs of every part; we muſt previouſly acquire
a true and perfect notion of the real deſign of
religion in general ; and then confider the
fitneſs and propriety of its ſeveral diſpenſa-
tions to promote and accompliſh that deſign,
through the various ſtates and conditions of
the world.   For it is from the ſtate and condition, that is, from the moral exigences of
mankind, that revelation takes its riſe : and
it is to the nature of theſe exigencies that
its contents are adapted.   And therefore it
muſt be from a comparative view of both
together, that the reaſonableneſs and excellency of any diſpenſation can be rightly deduced and illuſtrated.

Now, ſuch a comparative view of the
ſtates of the world, and the revealed diſ-
penſations connected with them, the Scripture faithfully exhibits to us; and thereby
ſupplies us with a proper clue, to trace the
beauties, and to unfold the wiſdom, of this
mighty, ſtupendous plan.

If then we conſult the Scripture-account,
it will manifeſtly appear, that, whilſt man
preſerved his original ſtate, and acted up to

his

his natural abilities, the government of the world went on, as we might expect, in a regular and uniform manner—without interruption, deviation or change. For what need of any alterations, or extraordinary interpofitions, when the firft man, under the guidance of his Creator, as a fon under the tuition of his father, might by the eftablifhed courfe of things, attain to that knowledge, virtue and happinefs, for which he was originally defigned?

But he perverfely forfook the guide of his life, and vainly fet up for his own director; in confequence of which, he not only fell far below the ftandard of his nature, but funk into the depth of mifery and woe. Now if God, in his goodnefs, determined to raife this fallen and corrupted man to his primitive ftation; much more if he defigned to advance him to higher degrees of virtue and happinefs, than what could be attained by the pre-eftablifhed laws of nature; it is obvious to conclude, that he muft neceffarily effect it by fome fupernatural method.

The

The conftitution and courfe of nature was originally adapted to the ftate of inno- cence; and contained no remedy for evils, occafioned by voluntary defection. Thefe, if remedied at all, muft be remedied by a fuperior hand; and in a way different from the original eftablifhment. Accordingly we find, that, when God came down to judge the offenders, but, at the fame time, with the kind intention of refcuing them at laft from the mifery and ruin they had brought upon themfelves; he fhewed this intention, as the cafe required, by an extraordinary exertion of knowledge and power—by pro- phecy and miracle: by prophecy firft, to open to the view of difconfolate man a new profpect of happinefs, and to rekindle in his breaft new hopes; and then by miracle, to ftrengthen and confirm thofe hopes in him, and to affure him of their future comple- tion.

The *promife*, thus made and confirmed, brought to our firft parents feafonable relief, and placed them again under the guidance of religion. But here it is to be obferved,

that,

that, as their character was now become more complicated, (for we are to confider them not only as men, but alfo as finners) fo their religion became of courfe proportionably complex likewife.

As *men*, or rational beings, they were ftill fubject to the religion of nature, and the law of reafon: they were ftill bound to entertain a right knowledge of God, and to pay him fincere, unfeigned obedience.

But as *finners*, admitted into a covenant of grace, they were moreover to profefs, according to the tenour of that covenant, a right faith in the promifed Redeemer; through the merits of whom the fincerely obedient were to be reftored to happinefs.

True religion then, on the eftablifhment of the new œconomy after the *fall*, confifted of thefe two parts—which it concerns us conftantly to bear in mind, as of great importance in our future inquiries.

Now, had the fucceeding generations retained this religion pure and incorrupt in both its parts, and lived up to the meafure of its obligations; the adminiftration of divine

vine government would probably have proceeded in its ufual courfe, without any
farther deflections.

But this, alas! was very far from being
the cafe. Mankind in a fhort time corrupted
their ways: and not only forgot the promife
of a Redeemer; but even funk into a deplorable ignorance of the one true God; and
plunged themfelves into an endlefs variety of
deftructive errours, and fatal fuperftitions.

When they had thus degenerated into
idolatry and wickednefs, and were in no-
wife able to reform themfelves; the prefervation of their happinefs manifeftly required,
that Providence fhould interpofe in fome extraordinary manner, to recall them to the
knowledge of thefe neceffary articles, and to
awaken them into a fenfe of their duty. Accordingly we are informed in the courfe of
this hiftory, that God did actually interpofe,
" at fundry times, and in diverfe manners, q"
for this purpofe; and marvelloufly conducted,
through a long period, two different kinds
of adminiftration together, adapted to the

q Heb. i. 1.

two

two different parts of religion, which they were intended to reftore.

But, as faith in God is the fundamental principle of all religion, fo the firft thing neceffary to be done for the recovery of mankind, was to bring them back to the belief and acknowledgement of that firft article, relating to his being and providence. " For he that cometh to God, muft believe that he is, or exifts; and that he is a rewarder of them, that diligently feek him [r]."

Conformably to this, the Scripture affures us, that thofe wonderful manifeftations fo frequently difplayed in the firft ages of the world, were chiefly defigned to convince the nations, of the falfhood and vanity of the opinions they had imbibed; and to render them fenfible, that Jehovah, the author of thofe amazing wonders, was the only great and true God;—and confequently, that He alone was intitled to their fervice and obedience. And it is one principal part of my defign in the following Difcourfes, to fhew how wifely thofe wondrous manifeftations

[r] Heb. xi. 6.

were

were contrived, and how properly they were adapted, to promote and accomplifh the end in view:—to fhew, how the doctrines and miracles confpired together, to difpel the darknefs of fuperftition and idolatry ; and to reftore mankind to the clear knowledge of their God and Creator.

But befides this, and in conjunction with it, there runs through the Old Teftament another fcheme of divine adminiftration, relative to the *fecond* article ; admirably fitted to fupport the hopes, and to confirm the faith of thofe, who lived under that Teftament, in the future advent of the promifed Redeemer. This fcheme has been fo happily unfolded, and fo fully explained by a late learned Prelate, in his Difcourfes on *The Ufe and Intent of Prophecy*, that I have only to obferve, how effectually it anfwered the purpofe of Providence ; as it raifed in the world a general expectation of the Meffiah's coming; and prepared the people for the reception of their Lord.

When the world, and particularly that nation which was the grand depofitary of true religion, was fo far enlightened by thefe adminiftrations, as to be thoroughly convinced, that Jehovah was the only God; and that, " in remembrance of his mercy, he was about to raife up a mighty falvation for them, as he had fpoken by the mouth of his holy prophets[s];" then it feems to be the proper time for the promifed Redeemer to make his appearance, in order to inftruct them in the will of God; and to direct them to thofe acts of real and fubftantial virtue, which are well-pleafing and acceptable to him.

And the event was exactly anfwerable. For the Gofpel affures us, that Jefus Chrift did accordingly appear " in the fulnefs of time[t];" the time appointed by the prophecies: that he made a clear and full declaration of God's will to mankind; and eftablifhed a more perfect inftitution of religion; the obfervance of which is to fecure to us the favour of God; and to entitle us, through the merits of this bleffed Redeemer,

[s] Luke i. 66. 70.
[t] Gal. iv. 4.

to

to the poffeffion of eternal happinefs.   And
it is another branch of my defign to fhew—
how well the doctrines, which Chrift delivered, were accommodated to the neceffities, and fitted for the moral improvement,
of the world: and alfo, how exquifitely the
miracles he wrought, were adjufted to evince
the truth of his doctrines: and confequently
to fhew, how fully both in conjunction
prove him to be " that prophet, that fhould
come into the world ª."

Thefe are the outlines of the plan, which
I have formed for myfelf in the prefent undertaking; and which I fhall endeavour gradually to fill up.

But to fill it up in a regular order, and fet
forth the feveral parts of it in their true and
proper light; it will be requifite to look back
to the creation of the world ; to contemplate
and confider the primitive ftate of mankind,
and the provifion that was originally made
for their happinefs.   And if this provifion,
which God had eftablifhed in the conftitution
of nature, and which he difpenfed by the or-

ª John vi. 14.

D 2   dinary

dinary courfe of things, appears to have been fuitable to the ftate and condition they were *then* in; we may reafonably prefume, that all the fubfequent difpenfations of his providence, though frequently of an extraordinary and miraculous kind, were planned and conducted with equal wifdom ; and were perfectly adapted to the various neceffities, which they *afterwards* laboured under.

But indeed, we have fomething more than prefumption, we have evident proof, to build upon. For, if we purfue the footfteps of mankind, as they paffed through the feveral periods of the world ; and examine the circumftances which they fell into from time to time; we fhall find the difpenfations, difplayed at thofe times, and in reference to thofe circumftances, to have been as full fraught with wifdom, as they were with goodnefs : to have been entirely fubfervient to the grand purpofe of human happinefs : and fubfervient to it in the very ways and methods, which feem, of all others, the moft proper to produce it.

This

'This we shall hereafter endeavour to shew from a distinct confideration of particulars. Suffice it at prefent to obferve, that the general view, which we have already taken of thefe difpenfations, exhibits a ftrong, general proof of what we have advanced concerning them.

If mankind were fo far funk into ignorance and errour, as to deify the feveral parts of nature, and " to worfhip the creatures inftead of the Creator[x];" what method more fuitable, proper and reafonable, could the Almighty make ufe of, to convince them of their folly, and bring them back to the obedience of himfelf; than that of counteracting the laws of nature, and miraculoufly controuling its operations and effects?—whereby they might fee, that to Him alone, as governor of the world, their veneration fhould, in prudence and juftice, be directed. For in thofe times of idolatry, the chief point to be fettled, was the fupremacy of Jehovah, and his government of the world. And therefore the far greater number of the

[x] Rom. i. 25.

D 3

miracles

miracles recorded in the Old Teftament, are directly applied to *this* point: and, being awakening inftances of terrible majefty, evidently prove—that the author of them was endowed with fupreme power; could bend the courfe of nature to his will; and was therefore to be revered, as the Lord and Governor of the whole earth.

When we come to the times of the New Teftament, we meet with miracles of a different kind; but no lefs properly adapted to the nature of the difpenfation, which they were wrought to atteft. Here God appears in milder majefty, inftituting a religion of perfect purity, and boundlefs love. Correfpondent therefore to the genius of this religion, the miracles performed for its fupport, are all miracles of mercy; which, at the fame time that they demonftrate the truth, breath forth the very fpirit and temper of the Gofpel. For the good will therein revealed towards mankind, is every where exemplified by the miraculous benefits conferred upon them. And what can we conceive more rational, convincing and fatisfactory,

than,

than that such a difpenfation—calculated to
remove the diforders of the *foul*, and to ·
advance it to a ftate of perfeⅽtion—fhould be
thus illuftrated, confirmed and eftablifhed,
by miracles which confift in curing the analogous difeafes of the *body*, and reftoring it
to perfeⅽt health?

Hence then may be difcovered the weaknefs and futility of this boafted objeⅽtion,
" that miracles can be no witnefs either for
God or men; nor are any proof either of divinity or revelation [y]." " For though," fay
our adverfaries, " innumerable miracles
fhould affail the fenfe, and give the trembling foul no refpite; though the fky fhould
fuddenly open, and all kinds of prodigies appear; voices be heard, or charaⅽters read;
yet, what would this evince, but only that
there were certain powers which could do all
this? But what powers; whether one or
more; whether fuperior or fubaltern; mortal or immortal; wife or foolifh; juft or unjuft; good or bad: this would ftill remain
a myftery; as would the true intention, the

[y] Charaⅽterifticks, vol. II. § 5. p. 331.

D 4   infal-

infallibility or certainty of whatever thefe
powers afferted [z]."

Now, in whatever ftate of myfterioufnefs
or obfcurity fingle miracles, confidered apart,
may leave thefe points involved; yet, miracles that run, as the Scripture-miracles do,
in one connected chain, are completely adapted to clear them up. For by this combination, this bond of union that fubfifts
between them, we may as eafily trace the
end and defign of thefe extraordinary effects,
as we can trace thofe of the ordinary works
of nature. And if we find, as we do find,
that they are all, though various, ftill cohe-
rent; that they are all fubfervient to fimilar
ends of wifdom and goodnefs, with thofe that
appear in the works of creation; that they
all co-operate to one common, benevolent
defign, the production of human happinefs;
then furely, " we have fufficient reafon to
conclude, and to be convinced, that they are
all the effects of *one* power—of one *fuperior*
and *immortal* power—of one power, *wife,*

[z] Characteriftics, vol. II. § 5. p. 333.

juft

juſt, and *good*[a] :" in a word, of *that* power, which firſt brought nature into being ; which then wiſely and gracjouſly eſtabliſhed laws for the happineſs of his creatures; and which afterwards, at times, as wiſely and gracjouſly counteracted thoſe laws, when it became neceſſary to their farther happineſs.

Here therefore is a clear diſplay—a full, irrefragable proof of *divine* power : and the *intention* of this power, in performing theſe marvellous works, is equally plain and obvious. For the nature of the miracles wrought, the relation they bear to the circumſtances of things, and the ſuitableneſs they diſcover to certain ends, are as clear indications of what the Almighty intended in the performance of them ; as the qualities and affections of natural bodies are indications of the deſign he had in view, when he produced thoſe bodies into being.

With reſpect to the miracles, wrought in confirmation of particular doctrines, they are ſo exquiſitely appropriated to the nature

a Brown's Eſſays on the Characteriſtics. Eſſay III. § IV. p. 276.

of

of thofe doctrines, as to be often real exem-
plifications of them. They are, in many
cafes, the very doctrines reduced into acts.
And the truth of fuch doctrines is as *certain*
and *infallible*, as it is *unqueſtionable* and *certain* that the acts were performed.

Upon the whole; the proofs of *final* caufes,
and confequently the proofs of the *intention*
of the Deity, are as vifible in the proceedings
that concern the *moral*, as in thofe that re-
late to the *natural* world. Natural bodies
neither ſtand more properly ranged, nor
operate more harmoniouſly to the ends of
creation ; than miracles do, to the purpofes
of revelation.

We fee them fpringing up, juſt at the
times, and exactly in the places, we might
reafonably expect: we fee them fucceeding
each other in a regular, connected order:
we fee them affuming various complexions,
according to the various neceffities and occafions, that called for them: we fee them,
completely anfwering . thofe occafions and
neceffities ; and thereby fecuring the happinefs of the world. And feeing all this, can
we

we poffibly doubt either the intent or propriety of them? can we poffibly doubt of
their being the genuine works of Him,
" who is excellent in wifdom, as well as
mighty in power;" and who, viewing the
end from the beginning, " fweetly ordereth
all the means [b]," that are neceffary to promote and accomplifh it?

If we fhould now try what effect it would
have, to fuppofe the order of the miracles
changed ; this would be a farther illuftration
both of the propriety of them, and of the
advantages refulting from their prefent fituation [c]. For which of the miracles exhibited
to Pharaoh would have been to Adam, what
the debafing of the ferpent to the abject ftate
of a reptile was—a ftanding fecurity for the
completion of his hopes, and a prelude to the
final overthrow of his enemy?

To what purpofe would the gift of languages have been conferred on the Ifraelites,
fecluded, as they were, from the converfe
and fociety of all foreign people?

[b] Wifd. viii. 1.
[c] ROTHERAM's Sketch, &c. § iii. p. 23.

Or

Or how would the power of defeating armies, and conquering nations by war, have promoted the eftablifhment of the Gofpel of peace? How would it have accorded with the genius and temper of that religion, whofe end is to level all diftinctions; to reduce mankind into one community; and to unite them in the bonds of charity and love?

-In the places they are fituated the miracles have all their ufe and beauty; the moment you tranfpofe them, their luftre is tarnifhed: their ferviceablenefs and propriety are no longer vifible; but the whole becomes at once an ufelefs and monftrous jumble of ftrange, confufed, unmeaning exertions.

Finally, as the order and difpofition of the miracles ferve thus to illuftrate and fet forth their *propriety*; fo do the circumftances under which they were exhibited, and the connection they maintain with the known natural ftate of the times, ferve to prove their *truth* and *reality*. They make, in the hiftory of thofe times, an effential part of the feveral events related: they are fo intimately inter-

woven

woven with the natural occurrences, that they cannot be feparated the one from the other, without violence : they are the auxiliaries of nature for the accomplifhment of the divine purpofes: they are indeed the very means that Providence made ufe of—and the only means that feem adapted—to work the reformation, and carry on the improvement of the world. Their exiftence therefore may be clearly deduced from the manifeft *improvement*, which mankind are allowed to have made in religious knowledge and moral practice.   In a word, the Jewifh and Chriftian religions, the grand inftruments of this improvement, were refpectively founded on the Jewifh and Chriftian miracles ; without which, they could never have been eftablifhed. Hence then, we are as fure, that thefe miracles were actually performed, and had a real exiftence ; as we are fure, that thefe religions now fubfift, and are profeffed in the world. And greater fecurity than this, no man, I think, can reafonably defire.

But, notwithftanding the force of this evidence, the incredulity of the prefent age has

has not only dared to call in queftion the *reality* of thefe miracles; but has proceeded fo far, as even to deny the *poffibility* of them. The validity of the reafonings, by which our adverfaries would fain reject them, I fhall bring to the teft in my next Difcourfe. In the mean time, convinced as we are, that " the foundation of God ftandeth fure[d];" that the religion which he eftablifhed by fuch a train of miracles, is infallibly true and divine; let us ferioufly attend to its important doctrines; and diligently endeavour to frame our lives according to its wife and excellent precepts. Let us fedately reflect, that the great end of all true religion, and more particularly of the Chriftian religion, is to reform its profeffors from vice and immorality; and to render them " zealous of good works[e]." When it influences our conduct in this manner, the benevolent defign of our Lord in revealing it, and the great intention of God in the miraculous atteftation he has been pleafed to give it, is effectually com-

[d] 2 Tim. ii. 19.
[e] Tit. ii. 14.

pleted.

pleted. Our falvation is begun; as, by the
forfaking of our fins, the caufes of our mifery
are removed. " And being made free from
fin [f]," the higher we advance in piety and
goodnefs, the better we fhall be difpofed for
the enjoyment of that happinefs, which
God has prepared for them that obey
him. To whom, with the Son and Holy
Ghoft, be afcribed all honour, adoration and
praife, &c. *Amen.*

[f] Rom. vi. 18.

SERMON III.

GEN. xviii. 14.

Is any thing too hard for the Lord?

AS miracles are such clear, positive and direct proofs of the truth of revelation; it is no wonder, that the patrons of infidelity should labour so industriously, in every age, to decry, explode and reject them. But of all the attempts that were ever made in any age to this purpose; one of the most subtile, as well as the most insolent, is that of a certain modern writer; who not only presumes to question the reality, but magisterially denies the possibility of miracles : who pronounces them to be in their own nature utterly incredible; and, when produced in support of any religious system, to be more

properly

properly a fubject of derifion than of argument [g].

But how light and ridiculous foever this
fubject may appear in the apprehenfion of
our faftidious author; it has certainly too
much weight, ftrength and ftability to be
puffed away by the mere arrogance of an in-
fulting farcafm. It is a ferious fubject, and
admits of argument. And therefore we fhall
affume the confidence, notwithftanding his
fcoffs, to argue the point with this contemp-
tuous adverfary: not indeed with any view
of working the conviction of fo prejudiced a
perfon; but in hopes of fecuring the better
difpofed, but lefs learned, from being led
away by the fophiftry of his reafonings.

And to this end, I fhall endeavour to
prove, in direct oppofition to the general
defign and avowed purport of his Tenth
Effay,

That miracles are fo far from being in their
own nature either impoffible or incredible;
that, on the contrary, there is ftrong pre-

g Hume's Effays, vol. II. § x. on Miracles, p. 139. 8vo.
Ed. 1767.

sumption,

fumption, nay, irrefragable evidence of their having been actually performed; and performed too in fupport and attestation of revealed religion.

In difcuffing thefe points I fhall proceed as the nature of the fubject directs; and attempt, in the

Firft place, to evince and demonftrate the *poffibility* of miracles.

The Almighty, when he created this vifible world, difpofed the parts of it in fuch order, and impreffed upon them fuch motions, as were adapted to accomplifh the gracious ends, which he propofed to himfelf in the creation of it. Now, as thefe ends, he forefaw, were in general attainable by one uniform mode of proceeding; fo he determined, that a conftant fucceffion of effects fhould uniformly proceed from their refpective caufes, according to certain ftated rules. Thefe rules, which natural bodies obferve in their operations, are commonly called the *laws of nature.* But the laws of nature are in reality the laws of God: that is, they are nothing elfe but the *modes of acting,* which

E 2 the

the wifdom of the Deity has prefcribed to
his power, in the prefervation and government of the natural world. For matter,
having no felf-determining principle, is,
properly fpeaking, capable of no law. Being
in itfelf inert and paffive, it can only act, as
it is acted upon. And therefore the courfe
of the material world ftands in need of the
fame power to continue it on, as was neceffary at firft to put it in motion. And indeed, fuch power is conftantly employed
upon it. For the principle of *gravitation*,
the moft extenfive and operative principle in
nature, is evidently no other than the continual agency of God[h].

Since the courfe of nature, then, is nothing
elfe but that continued uniform manner, in
which God produces certain effects according
to his own wifdom ; and fince this manner
of acting depends entirely upon his wifdom ;
he may at any time, if he fees fit, as eafily
alter it, as he may continue it : in other

[h] NEWTONI Principia, &c. lib. III. prop. XLII. fchol. gen.
See alfo MACKLAURIN's Account of Sir I. NEWTON's Difcove-
ries, b. IV. ch. IX. § 1. 5. 6. 13. and PRICE's Diſſert. on Providence, § 2.

words,

words, he may as eafily work a miracle, and
" perform a *new* thing [i]" in the earth, as
he may perfevere in the *old*, common way,
and keep things on in their ordinary courfe.
For the ordinary and extraordinary are
equally in his power, and equally fubject to
his will and controul. For no man will
contend, that it requires more or greater
power to ftop or alter the motions of the
planets, than it does to carry them round in
their orbits. No man will contend, that it
requires a greater power to deluge the earth,
or to divide the fea, than it did at firft to
create them; and does ftill to preferve them in
their prefent ftate. No man will contend, that
it requires a greater power to reftore life to a
body when dead, than to give life to a body
that before never lived. Or, if any one
fhould be difpofed to contend thefe points;
yet he cannot deny, but that infinite power
is able to perform them.

Hence then it follows, that miracles are
poffible; that the Ruler of the world *may*
counteract the laws, or alter the courfe of it,

[i] Numb. xvi. 30.

E 3   when

when he fees proper. But when it may be proper for him to act in fuch a manner, WE are not always competent judges. This however we may judge, that in general and common cafes, he will always act according to the general and common courfe of things: as that courfe will be fufficient to anfwer the great and ultimate end of all his actions—the production of the common and general good.

But, to come to my *fecond* point,

If any *extraordinary* occafions fhould arife, which require extraordinary provifions; then it is *probable* that he will make thofe provifions for them in fome extraordinary way: that is, he will *probably* perform miracles. For MIRACLES ARE EXTRAORDINARY EF-FECTS PRODUCED UPON EXTRAORDINARY OCCASIONS. And that fuch occafions *may* arife, both in the natural and moral world, 'tis an eafy matter to conceive. In the natural world, the *attraction* of bodies may bring on fuch irregularities, as can no otherwife be adjufted, than by the hand of Him who firft formed it [k]. And in the moral

---

[k] NEWTON's Optics, Query 31. p. 378.

world,

world, the *corruption* of free agents may occafion fuch enormities, as can only be recti-
fied by the interpofition of Providence.

In fuch circumftances therefore, where it
feems necefiary that God, both as preferver
and governor of the world, *fhould* interpofe
for its fupport and welfare ; it is very probable he *may* have interpofed : and more efpecially in matters relating to true religion.
For fince he is peculiarly concerned for the
happinefs, and, as the means of it, for the
moral improvement, of mankind ; if men,
by a wrong ufe of their liberty, fhould
plunge themfelves into vice and wretched-
nefs : if, in that ftate of ignorance and
errour, inftead of being able to recover themfelves, they fhould continually fink into ftill
worfe and worfe condition : what can you
conceive more *probable*, than that God fhould
interpofe, by fome fignal act of his providence, to reclaim them to the practice of
virtue and religion ; and thereby reftore
them to the capacity of attaining that happinefs, for which they were originally defigned?

If

"If real piety and moral virtue, with the religious knowledge that is neceffary to them, are objects worthy of the divine attention; and if thefe were in danger of perifhing utterly out of the world; " why fhould it be thought a thing incredible, that God" fhould commiffion proper perfons to republifh the doctrines, and enforce the duties of religion and morality, with clear and exprefs authority? This commiffion of the prophets would be in itfelf miraculous: but then the miracle would not appear openly to the world: and therefore fome *other* miracles, *obvious* and *fenfible*, would be neceffary to atteft its truth. Superior knowledge and virtue are not alone fufficient to characterize a prophet. He muft alfo " do fuch things, as no man can do, except God were with him," before his prophetic character will be eftablifhed, and himfelf be acknowledged as a divine teacher[l]. And therefore we may conclude, that every prophet, employed upon any extraordinary meffage, would be endowed with this power of

[l] See Dr. Adams's Effay on Miracles, p. 33.

working

working miracles, as well in confirmation of his own miffion, as in fupport of the doctrines he had in charge to teach [m].

And if it fhould appear from the hiftory of the world, that fuch good ends have in fact been anfwered by them: if it fhould appear, for example, that religion and morality, when juft expiring, had been revived by the help of thefe miracles; had been eftablifhed among feveral nations; and in a way likely to gain farther ground: this will be a ftrong prefumption in their favour. And if it fhould farther appear, that there is no other affignable caufe, which could bring about this great event, but the miracles recorded to have been wrought for the purpofe; this will be a good proof, that they *were* accordingly wrought; and actually performed with that intention [n].

What a ftrange conduct therefore muft it be in our adverfary, to allow that " miracles may be *poffible*; nay, and *probable* too; provided they have nothing to do with religion."

[m] STILLINGFLEET's Origin. Sacræ, b. II. ch. vi. § 15.
[n] ADAMS's Effay, p. 34.

For where fhould we expect them to be
employed, but on objects worthy of them?
And what objects can we conceive of fuch
dignity and importance, as thofe which religion exhibits? If God then can be thought
to have any regard for the things that concern the tranfient enjoyments of this *mortal*
life; how much greater attention may he
be fuppofed to pay, to the things that refpect
our *immortal* ftate? But thefe are the things
of religion: the things that make for the
fupreme intereft of mankind, through time,
and through eternity. From hence then,
from the dignity and importance of their
defign, there arifes a *peculiar* prefumption in
favour of fuch miracles, as are faid to have
been wrought in fupport of religion °.

"No, fays the infidel;" and retorts upon
us—"if there be any prefumption, that
miracles were wrought in *former* times, to
fupport the doctrines, and enforce the practice
of true religion; there muft fubfift, of courfe,
an equal prefumption, that they would ftill

° CAMPBELL's Differtation on Miracles, § V. p. 89, &c.
Bp. BUTLER's Anal. of Religion, pt. ii. ch. ii. p. 243, &c,

be

be performed in our *own* times, for the fame ends—becaufe religion and morality want ftill to be propagated,—ftill to be enforced in the world. And fince it is certain, that God performs no miracles *now* for that purpofe; the prefumption is, from the rules of analogy, that he *never* did perform any."

Now, in anfwer to this, let it here be obferved, that it is in no wife neceffary, as the inference would fuppofe, to keep always to the fame method, in order to accomplifh the fame end. We learn from the conftitution of nature, that it requires far greater care, pains and trouble, to fettle, ftrengthen, and eftablifh things at *firft*, than it does *afterwards* to preferve and fupport them: in time indeed, they may be able to preferve and fupport themfelves. Hence then, if no miracles are wrought at prefent for the propagation of religion, the reafon is plain— religion may be propagated without them. And God will never be fo lavifh of his power, as to make ufe of extraordinary

means,

means, when common and ordinary ones are found sufficient.

But though common and ordinary means are sufficient *now*; yet, in the *beginning* they were not so. For true religion, like a tender plant, required, when first set in the earth, to be watered and nourished with the dew of heaven; without which it would have withered away. It required to be guarded with constant care; to be defended from all annoyances; and to be fortified against the violence of all the storms, that might fall and beat upon it. It required therefore the peculiar attention of Providence, and the signal exertion of his mighty arm: that is, it required miracles to be wrought in its favour, in order both to promote its success, and to secure its establishment in the world. When afterwards, in consequence of such miraculous interpositions, " it had taken root, and filled the land ʳ;" when it had been widely diffused, and sufficiently established among the nations; then indeed might it safely be left to preserve itself; and to make its way

ʳ Psalm lxxx. 9.

7

by

by its own strength, without any special affistance.

This is the conclusion we are led to form from the analogy of nature; and is a conclusion that stands fully confirmed by the evidence of facts. For if experience tells us, that God *now* acts in the affairs of religion according to the *natural* course of things: and, having committed it to the care and management of its professors, leaves it to the influence and result of their conduct: so history assures us, on the other hand, that in *ancient* times he acted in a *different* manner; that he watched over religion with a providential eye; attended to its various states and conditions; and, as occasions required, succoured, supported, strengthned, stablished it by frequent and *supernatural* displays of his power. Which brings me, in the

Third place, To prove the *reality* and *certainty* of miracles.

There are two religions now in the world—the *Jewish* and the *Christian*—which, though they sprung up under the most un-

promising

promifing afpect, yet made their way with furprifing fuccefs. If we compare the genius of thefe religions with the temper and difpofitions of the times, we fhall find that they contain nothing, that was particularly adapted to engage the *affections*, but much that might eafily excite the *averfion*, of a loofe and degenerate world. For the burdenfome ceremonies of the former were no lefs ungrateful to the *indolence*, than the fublime purity of the latter was to the *corruption*, of depraved nature. But, notwithftanding the prejudices that lay againft them, and the oppofition that was made to them, thefe religions ftill prevailed; and gained, in their day, an extenfive reception among mankind. But by what means did they gain it? Not by natural, but by fupernatural means: by the help of the miracles, that were publicly performed to atteft their truth. Thefe miracles the people faw; and believed the revelations confirmed by them. And this their profefted belief of the one, is an irrefragable proof of the reality of the other.

But

But this evidence will appear in a ftronger light, if we confider the relation, which thefe miracles bear to the ftate and circum-ftances of the times; and the connection they maintain with the known fituation of things. When we examine the miracles recorded by heathen authors, we cannot but obferve, that they are all detached events, and properly make no part of the hiftory; fince the fame feries of affairs might be carried on, and the fame ends be accomplifhed, as well without the interpofition of them, as with it: and therefore may conclude, that they were pur-pofely introduced, either to enliven a dull narration, or to anfwer fome bafe, political defign.   But the Scripture-miracles are of a different ftamp.   They plainly conftitute an *effential* part of the feveral events related: and are fo intimately interwoven with the natu-ral occurrences, that they cannot be fepa-rated from them.   They all work to fome rational, important end; and come in, oppor-tunely, to affift and ftrengthen the weaknefs of nature, in order to bring that end about. Take away the affiftance of miracles, in the

cafes

cafes they are faid to have been wrought, and you will inftantly perceive, that nature *muft* fink under the weight of the tranfactions; and that, her powers being unequal to the work, the œconomy of the times muft come to a dead ftand. Miracles only could carry it on: nor is there any fuch thing, as proceeding fcarce a ftep without them.

Place the *Jews,* as they *were* placed, in *Egypt*; and who will you bring them out, againft the will of their tyrannical mafters, unlefs by a miracle performed in their favour? Then, obferve their embarrafment at the *Red fea*; and think, how it is poffible, without *another* miracle, to deliver them from the fury of their enraged enemies, and land them fafe on the oppofite fhore? Attend them afterwards in their journeyings through the wildernefs, for the fpace of forty years; and how were they to be fuftained, for fo long a time, in that barren defart, without a feries of *conftant* miracles? Then, bring them to the borders of the land of *Canaan*; and how, I befeech you, could they poffibly expel the inhabitants of this land, and get

poffeffion

poffeffion of it themfelves, without the affiftance of his arm, "who ruleth over all
the kingdoms of the earth," and difpofeth of
them "according to the purpofe of his own
will?" Here therefore He introduced them;
and here He protected them, whilft they
"kept his ftatutes, and obferved his laws."

But the *Jewifh* law was only an introduction to that nobler inftitution, which
was eftablifhed by Chrift, as the other had
been by Mofes, on the foundation of ap-
propriate miracles. For what but the *reality*
of the miracles, which our Saviour performed
in proof of his doctrines, could prevail on
fuch a number of people, naturally prejudiced the contrary way, to become his difciples; and, under the weight and preffure
of fo many hardfhips, fteadily to embrace
and profefs his religion? And what but the
reality of the miracles, which thefe difciples
again were enabled to work, could fo effectually recommend it to the acceptance of
others? For many and many others did accept and embrace it, on the evidence of the
miracles, which *they* faw performed in at-

teftation

teftation of it: and thereby declared to the world, that they were fully convinced of the *truth* and *certainty* of thofe miracles. And this their declaration ought to be credited: not only as the teftimony of fo many witneffes fhould in reafon be deemed valid ; but as it alfo fupplies us with a clear and fatisfactory account of events, which otherwife are unaccountable [q]. For admit the miracles to be true ; and all the events, recorded both in the *Old* and *New* Teftament, are juft what we fhould have expected to follow : but reject them as falfe ; and we are inftantly involved in difficulties and perplexities; and obliged at laft to believe things, in their own nature, much more incredibl, or, as our author fpeaks, "much more miraculous, than even the miracles themfelves."

But all this, it is faid, ftands upon teftimony : "and no teftimony for any kind of miracle can ever amount to a *probability*, much lefs to a *proof*; or even fuppofing it amounted to a proof, it would be oppofed by another proof, derived from the very na-

[q] See Butler's Analogy, part II. chap. ii. p. 352, &c.

ture

ture of the fact which it would endeavour to
eftablifh.   'Tis experience only which gives
authority to human teftimony ; and 'tis the
fame experience, which affures us of the
laws of nature. When, therefore, thefe two
kinds of experience (obferve the words) are
contrary, we have nothing to do but fub-
tract the one from the other, and embrace
an opinion, either on one fide or the other,
with that affurance, which arifes from the
remainder.   But, according to the principle
here explained, this fubtraction, with regard
to all popular religions, amounts to an intire
annihilation : and therefore we may eftablifh
it as a maxim, that no human teftimony
can have fuch force as to prove a miracle ;
and make it a juft foundation for any fuch
fyftem of religion [r]."

   This is the mighty argument, by which
Mr. Hume would overturn at once all the
miracles recorded in Scripture.   But this, in
truth, is fo far from being an *argument*, that
it is nothing more than down-right fophiftry ; the moft fallacious reafoning that was

ever ufed. And the fallacy lies in this :——
that he takes the proofs from teftimony in
fupport of miracles, and the proofs from experience in fupport of the eftablifhed courfe
of nature, to be direct *contrary* proofs:
whereas, in reality, they have no relation
to each other; but refpect quite different
facts. The unformity of nature is in no
wife contradicted by the fuppofition of miracles. Nay, by fuppofing the facts in
queftion to be miraculous, the uniformity
of nature is preferved, and the facts are accounted for upon another principle entirely
confiftent with it [s]. All that common experience proves, is, that there is a fettled
courfe of nature; and that, in *common* and
ordinary cafes, things proceed according to
this fettled courfe. But with regard to *ex-*
traordinary occafions, experience can determine nothing. For *them*, we muft have re-
courfe to the hiftory of the times in which
they happened; and fee what the men of
thofe times have related and vouched concerning them : and if we find that they una-

* Dr. ADAMS's Effay, p. 17.

nimoufly

nimoufly teftify, that on fuch *extraordinary*
occafions *extraordinary* or *miraculous* things
were performed; miracles truly worthy of
God, and fuitable to the neceffities that
called for them; then are we bound in
reafon to receive this their teftimony " with
full affurance of faith." I fay, with *full*
affurance; becaufe there is nothing that can
tend to diminifh it. For it is in the higheft
degree abfurd, to talk of *fubtracting* the evidence of experience from the evidence of
this teftimony—fince they are evidences of
different facts, and therefore incapable of
being compared together [t].

[t] " If miracles, fays Bifhop BUTLER, muft be compared to any
thing in nature, they fhould not be compared to common natural events, or to events, which, though uncommon, are fimilar
to what we daily experience; but to the extraordinary phæno-
mena of nature. And then the comparifon will be between the
prefumption againft miracles, and the prefumption againft fuch
uncommon appearances——Upon which he concludes, that
there is certainly no fuch prefumption againft miracles, as to
render them in any wife incredible: that, on the contrary, our
being able to difcern reafons for them, gives a pofitive credibility to the hiftory of them, in cafes where thefe reafons hold."
Analogy, part II. ch. ii. p. 245, &c. See alfo Dr. PRICE's
Differt. on Hiftorical Evidence and Miracles.

But

But if our author fhould fail to make the *fubtraction* in this form; he is refolved, however, to make it in another. And therefore tells us, " that there is not to be found, in all hiftory, any miracle attefted by a fufficient number of men, of fuch unqueftioned good fenfe, education, and learning, as to fecure us againft all delufion in themfelves; of fuch undoubted integrity, as to place them beyond all fufpicion of any defign to deceive others; of fuch credit and reputation in the eyes of mankind, as to have a great deal to lofe, in cafe of being detected in any falfhood; and, at the fame time, attefting facts, performed in fuch a public manner, and in fo celebrated a part of the world, as to render the detection unavoidable: all which circumftances, he fays, are requifite to give us a full affurance in the teftimony of men [u]."

Very well. And have not *all* thefe requifites been over and over fhewn to concur in fupport of the Scripture-miracles? Thefe

---

[u] Hume's Effays ubi fupra.

miracles

miracles " were not done in a corner[x]."
they did not make their firft appearance in
fuch a place as Paphlagonia, a land of bar-
barity and dulnefs; where our author's favourite, Alexander, the impoftor, began his
feats; but they fhone forth in the moft
celebrated parts of the world, and at the
moft celebrated periods. Egypt, Phœnicia,
and Canaan faw them, believed and trembled:
Babylon, Jerufalem, Athens, Rome and Co-
rinth were all eye-witneffes of them; and
ftand upon record as vouchers for their truth
and certainty. Nor were they only performed in fuch renowned places, but they
were alfo performed in direct oppofition to
the prejudices and intereft of the moft renowned and powerful in thofe places. They
were performed before the moft vigilant,
acute and malicious enemies; who vigo-
roufly exerted all their induftry, fkill and
fagacity in the examination of them; and
who, if they had been falfe, would certainly
have detected the impofture. The teftimony
given to thefe miracles, was given in the

[x] Acts xxvi. 26.

F 4

fame

same places, and in the same public manner, by an infinite number of men; men of
cool reason and sound judgement; neither
heated by enthusiasm, nor fired by ambition;
but sedate in their conduct, and humble in
their pursuits; men, who were uniform in
their account of things; and who, not only
" took joyfully the spoiling of their goods ^y,"
but patiently endured all the hardships of
persecution and death, for the sake of what
they attested : and consequently men, who
thereby gave to the world the higheft proof,
that could poffibly be given *by men*, of the
truth and fidelity of their teftimony?

Nor is it any diminution of the force of
this argument, or any prejudice to the caufe
it maintains, that miracles have been forged,
and ftrenuoufly fupported by perfons of other
religions. " The forgeries of this fort, which
have been impofed upon mankind in all ages,
are fo far from weakening the credibility of
the Jewifh and Chriftian miracles, that they
ftrengthen it. For how could we account
for a practice fo univerfal, of forging mi-

y Heb. x. 34.

racles

racles for the fupport of falfe religions; if, on fome occafions, they had not actually been wrought for the confirmation of a true one? or, how is it poffible, that fo many fpurious copies fhould pafs upon the world, without fome genuine original from which they were drawn, whofe known exiftence and tried fuccefs might give an *appearance* of probability to the counterfeit? Now, of all the miracles of antiquity, there are none that can *pretend* to the character of originals, but thofe of the Old and New Teftament; which, though the oldeft by far of all others now recorded in the world, have yet maintained their credit to this day, through the perpetual oppofition and fcrutiny of ages; whilft all the rival productions of fraud and craft have long ago been fuccef- fively exploded, and funk into utter con- tempt.—An event that cannot reafonably be afcribed to any other caufe, but to the na- tural force and effect of truth; which, though defaced for a time by the wit, or depreffed by the power, of man, is fure ftill to

triumph

triumph in the end over all the falſe mi-
mickry of art, and the vain efforts of human policy [z]."

Now to God the Father, &c.

---

[z] Dr. MIDDLETON's Letter from Rome, Pref. Diſcourſe, p. 88.

S E R-

S E R M O N IV.

GEN. iii. 14, 15.

And the Lord God faid unto the ferpent,
Becaufe thou haft done this, thou art curfed
above all cattle, and above every beaft of the
field; upon thy belly fhalt thou go, and duft
fhalt thou eat all the days of thy life.

And I will put enmity between thee and the
woman, and between thy feed and her feed: it
fhall bruife thy head, and thou fhalt bruife
his heel.

HAVING already proved in a former
Difcourfe, that the great Ruler of the
world might, if he faw fit, counteract or
alter the courfe of nature; and, that it was
probable

probable he would accordingly do it, if the happinefs of his creatures fhould ever call for fuch alterations; it becomes our bufinefs now to inquire,

Whether the circumftances of mankind were ever fuch, as to ftand in need of miraculous interpofitions?

And if they were,

Whether the miracles, recorded to have been done, were properly adapted in their nature and kind, to the neceffities and occafions of fuch circumftances?

If thefe two points can be rationally eftablifhed, the ufefulnefs and propriety of the Scripture-miracles will appear in a confpicuous light. And, if the internal characters of ufefulnefs and propriety may with juftice be attributed to them; we are then furnifhed, not only with an additional prefumption in favour of their credibility, but with a fufficient anfwer to the principal objections urged againft it. For moft of the objections, which infidels have raifed againft thefe miracles, are ultimately founded on their fuppofed inutility, impropriety, or un-reafon-

reafonablenefs. And all this unbelievers are pleafed to fuppofe of them, becaufe they view them in a detached light; in an uncon- nected ftate ; and independent of the occa- fions that gave rife to them. Whereas, if thefe fceptics were ferioufly to examine the moral circumftances of mankind, through the feveral periods of the world; they would find great and frequent neceffities · for fome fignal interpofitions to be made on their be- half, for the recovery, or the improvement, of their happinefs. And if they were duly to confider the nature and tendency of thofe interpofitions, which are faid to have been made, they would fee reafon, and good reafon, to admire the wifdom with which they are adapted to the ends propofed : and hence might haply be induced to acknow- ledge the hand of the Almighty in them ; and from this acknowledgement might be farther led to praife and adore him with humble gratitude, as well for his extraordi- nary, as for his ordinary works.

Let us therefore conduct them through thefe fcenes; and try if we can contribute

any

any thing to their conviction, by pointing out the intent and propriety of the feveral miracles, in the order they arife, and prefent themfelves to us.

In the beginning of the world, there feems to have been no occafion for any miracles; and therefore we read of none. For, as man was created in a ftate of uprightnefs, purity and innocence; he had nothing elfe to do to fecure his happinefs and the divine favour, but to perferve himfelf in that ftate, by "walking uprightly with his God." The circumftances of this condition, at this time, required only a proper rule of life, to direct him to fuch things as were perfectly agreeable to the divine will, and confequently beneficial to himfelf; and to guard him from the contrary, or things that were hurtful. And fuch a rule, we find, he had. For, as he held frequent and familiar communication with the Deity; had probably the *Shechinah*, the fymbol of the divine prefence, continually before his eyes, to which he might refort on every occafion [a]; fo he received from

---

[a] WINDER's Hift. of Knowl. vol. I. ch. iii. § 2. TAYLOR's Sch. of Script. Divinity, ch. xiv.

thence, as from a " lively oracle," a juft and
fufficient information of things ; and was accordingly directed either to the ufe or for-
bearance of them [b].   As long as he continued to follow this direction, fo long he
continued in a happy ftate.   Upon this plan,
he could know no evil ; for God would direct him to that which was good—and to
that only : and he was always at hand, ready
to give him the needful directions.

During this period then, whilft man
obeyed the commands of God, and acted
fuitably to the end of his creation; nothing
more feems to have been neceffary to maintain the welfare and happinefs of the world,
(nor does any thing more feem indeed to have
been done for that purpofe) than to preferve
the whole in its original ftate ; and to conduct it onwards according to its natural,
eftablifhed courfe.

How long this happy period lafted, we
know not: nor is it indeed material we
fhould.   But this we are fure of, that a vaft

[b] Gen. i. 28—30. Ibid. ii. 16, 17. Ibid. 23, 24, comp. with
Mat. xix. 5. Mar. x. 7. 1 Cor. vi. 16.

and momentous change was, in procefs of time, fuperinduced on the world by the tranfgreffion of our firft parents: and this change, in the nature and conftitution of things, occafioned as great and ftupendous a change in the mode of divine government. It was introduced thus—*Satan*, moved perhaps with envy at the happinefs of our progenitors in paradife, " took occafion from the commandment——YEA, HATH GOD SAID, &c. c to " deceive them ; and thereby flew them d :" that is, robbed them of their innocence; and brought them to a ftate of mifery and death.

Such was the tranfaction in general : but it makes too confiderable a part of our fubject to be difmiffed in fuch general terms; and therefore we fhall defcend to particulars. To effect his defign then, the feducer affumed the body of a ferpent e——a creature of

great

---

c Gen. iii. 1.

d Rom. vii. 11.

e That the ferpent was the vifible inftrument of feduction is evident; and yet, that the tempter was more than a ferpent,

even

great fubtilty'; and at that time of a noble
form ; far fuperior to that which he bears at
prefent. *This,* how little foever we may
have attended to it, the Scripture has been
careful to apprize us of: for in the account
before us, he is twice reckoned, and exprefly reckoned among the *beafts* [f], in plain
contradiftinction to *reptiles*. And his fagacity,
recorded as well known to man, feems alfo

even a reafonable, but wicked Being, is no lefs evident. Herein
all antiquity feems to have been agreed: and feveral traces of
this account are ftill to be feen in profane authors. To the inftances which Bifhop STILLINGFLEET has produced in his *Orig.
Sacr.* b. iii. ch. iii. § 17, 18. many others might eafily be added—What is *Ahariman*, the name of the evil *dæmon* among the
Perfians, but הערום *Haharum*, the *fubtile one*, mentioned in
this hiftory? or, to exprefs it more fully, What is 'Αριμάνης, or
'Αρειμάνιος of the *Greeks*, but the ערום נחש *Harum Na-
chafh*, the *fubtile ferpent* of MOSES? And whence came the account, fo frequent in heathen authors, of their *heroes*, the friends
and protectors of mankind, being bit by *ferpents*, and generally
in the *heel*, but from the clofe of this hiftory, as applied to the
Meffiah?—PHILO *Judæus* feems to me to have been the firft author that ever thought of reducing this hiftory to an allegory or
parable. The various opinions of Jews and Chriftians on this
fubject may be feen together in RIVINI Differt. de Serpente Se-
ductore. *Lipfiæ*, 1686.

[f] Gen. iii. 1 and 14.

VOL. I.   G   to

to imply, that he was familiar with man ;
and therefore a fitter inftrument of decep-
tion [g].

The fcene lies near the forbidden tree ; of
whofe fruit, it is evident, from the tenour of
the narration, the woman faw the ferpent
eat : and to his eating of it (affured as fhe
was of its being the tree of *knowledge*) fhe
attributed thofe perfections of fpeech and
reafon, with which fhe perceived him to be
now endowed : and therefore, was not fur-
prifed. Under the advantage of this notion
he affaults the woman, and invites *her* to
eat likewife : but fhe refufed, it feems, even
to touch it. Upon this refufal the ferpent
infults her with the following queftion ;
What, you refufe then to eat of this tree,
becaufe God hath faid, ye fhall not eat of
every tree of the garden [h] ?" obliquely infi-
nuating, that God was not fo gracious and
beneficent as they might think him ; fince
he had with-held fuch excellent and fuper-

g Mede's Works, b. i. dif. XL. p. 224.
h Gen. iii. 1.

                                        lative

lative fruit from them [i]. To this the woman, vindicating the benevolence and goodneſs of God, anſwers—" We may eat of the fruit of the trees of the garden: but of the fruit of the tree which is in the midſt of the garden, God hath ſaid, Ye ſhall not eat of it, neither ſhall ye touch it, leſt ye die [k]." This apprehenſion of death the ſerpent, or rather the tempter through the ſerpent, treats as an idle and weak notion; and accordingly ſaid unto the woman, " ye ſhall not ſurely die [l]." ' You may be certain from what you ſee in me, who have eaten of it, not to my hurt, but much to my advantage, that death is not the conſequence; and therefore cannot be the true reaſon, why you are forbidden it. If you are at a loſs to underſtand, why God, when the tree is not deſtructive, ſhould yet forbid you to eat of it; I will be ſo far your friend, as to acquaint you with the real ſecret—And it is this: God would keep you in ſubjection to himſelf; and therefore with-holds it from

[i] Vide Targ. in Gen. iii. 4.
[k] Gen. iii. 2, 3.
[l] Ib. 4.

you,' " becaufe he knows, that in the day
ye eat thereof, you will become your own
mafters: then your eyes will be opened,
and ye fhall be as gods, knowing good and
evil[m]." Here indeed the woman ought in
duty to have confulted God; but the argument, you may obferve, was fo artfully
framed, as effectually to prevent her applying to him: for fhe could never think of
confulting a Being, whom fhe fufpected of
impofing upon her[n]. She was confequently
left to the workings of her own mind; and
to determine the point by her own judgment.
And the refult was, as we might naturally
expect, that, " when the woman faw,"
from the ferpent's experiment, " that the tree
was good for food;" and from her own obfervation, " that it was pleafant to the eyes;
and," from the fame ferpent's account, " that
it was a tree to be defired to make one wife;—
fhe took of the fruit thereof—and did eat.[o]"

[m] Gen. iii. 5.

[n] See Abp. King's Sermon on the Fall of man, at the end of
" Origin of Evil." Law's Edition.

[o] Gen. iii. 6.

3

Thus

Thus fell Eve, beguiled by the ſerpent. Adam, it ſhould ſeem, fell in another manner. For in the apology, which he afterwards makes to God, he uſes theſe words—"the woman whom thou gaveſt to be with me, ſhe gave me of the tree, and I did eat[p]:" plainly, I think, intimating, that the ſtrong affection, which God had planted in his breaſt towards her; and ſtrengthened by the command, that "he ſhould cleave unto her[q];" had prompted and diſpoſed him "to obey her voice[r]," and to ſhare her fate.

And what is there now in this account of the *fall*, that is either abſurd, irrational, or incredible? Are not the wiſeſt of the ſons of Eve, and thoſe more eſpecially who laugh the loudeſt at this ſtory, continually deceived by the like methods? And is not their diſobedience an exact copy of the firſt ſin? But, we are not ſo much concerned to bring examples to explain the manner, as we are to

[p] Gen. iii. 12.
[q] Gen. ii. 24.
[r] Gen. iii. 17.

confider the effect and confequence, of this firft tranfgreffion.

And here we fee at one difmal view the whole world defaced[1], and man, the lord of the world, entirely ruined, by it. His title to the favour of God became extinct with his innocence; and the fame act, that loft him his happinefs, expofed him to the penalty of mifery. In this ftate of accumulated dif-trefs—defpoiled of his innocence, perfection and felicity; and fubjected to all the mife-ries of mortality—where, or to whom, could he look for relief? He had no help in himfelf: and the majefty of God was no longer an object of comfort, but, on the contrary, of difmay and of terrour to him[t]. Having no delight, no confidence in God, there could be no place for religion. And if religion once failed amidft all the miferies that crowded upon him; his next wifh muft certainly be, that life might fail him alfo.

Hence then it appears, that our diftreffed progenitor muft inevitably fink, unlefs fup-

[1] Gen. iii. 17, 18.
[t] Ibid. 10.

ported

ported by some rational hope : by the hope of recovering, at least in part, what he had lost by his transgression. But this hope could be given him only by that Being against whom he had transgressed. And therefore if God had mercy in store ; if he intended to preserve and relieve the offender ; it was absolutely necessary, that he should reveal so much of his intention to him, as might be sufficient to animate him with the hope of reconciliation, and excite his endeavours to better obedience. For, otherwise, he would have concluded, that God had rejected him ; and, in consequence thereof, would have either languished in a fruitless inactivity, or else have proceeded (which is the most likely) with the same desperation as the fallen angels.

Now, the promise then made, that " the feed of the woman should bruise the serpent's head ᵘ—" was made directly with this intent ; and manifestly conveyed such hopes to him. For, if we consider the genius of the *Hebrew* language, the circumstances of man's situa-

ᵘ Gen. iii. 15.

G 4

tion

tion at that time, and the inſtrument by which the tempter worked his ſeduction, miſery and ruin ;, we ſhall ſoon be convinced, that his reſtoration and recovery could hardly be expreſſed (preſerving the reference to the manner of his *fall*) in more lively and comprehenſive terms.

Nor could Adam fail of drawing this meaning from them. He knew full well, at this juncture, that his *fall* was the *victory* of the ſerpent; whom he had now diſcovered, by his own experience, to be an enemy to God and man. From this diſcovery he might be led to conclude, that the ſerpent was not the real agent; but ſome evil ſpirit, which had taken poſſeſſion of the ſerpent's body. And in this concluſion he muſt needs be confirmed by the ſentence he heard denounced againſt him. For it was directed to an intelligent and free agent; to one who had committed a crime, which a brute creature was not capable of committing ; and had incurred a puniſhment, which a mere paſſive inſtrument could not incur. Hence then he could not but infer, that the true

object

object of the divine vengeance was the evil
spirit, which had committed the offence [x].
And as soon as ever he comprehended this,
it was an easy matter to deduce the rest. The
head was another word for *power*; and so
used in his own language: and therefore he
could not but understand, that to " *bruise*
the *head* of the serpent," was to *destroy* the
power of that evil spirit, which had actuated
the organs of this creature, to his seduction
and misery. Hereupon his hopes would naturally revive. For the destruction of the
power of his adversary, evidently implied a
deliverance from those evils, which that
power had brought him under: and by consequence, a recovery of those blessings, which
he had forfeited by the *fall*. And this was
a sufficient foundation (which was all that
the necessity of his case required) for trust
and confidence in God; and a sufficient encouragement to the exercise of religion, and
to a stedfast obedience for the time to come.
I say, " stedfast obedience:" because he must
be sensible, that the happiness lost by sin,

[x] Revel. exam. with Candour, vol. I. Diss. v. p. 59, &c.

could

..y be recovered by the return of
:. ..oufnefs.

But, notwithftanding this promife, or rather prophecy, was fo full and exprefs; yet
our anxious progenitor (efpecially when he
found that it was to take place in one of his
pofterity) might ftand in need, and in great
need, of fome fign or miracle to affure him
of its completion ; and to comfort him with
the thoughts, that it carried a reference alfo
to himfelf. We have in Scripture frequent
inftances of *faithful* men requiring fome miraculous figns by way of fecurity for the accomplifhment of divine promifes; and we
have as frequent inftances of God's indul-
gence to their weaknefs in granting them
fuch figns [y]. And would not the fame folicitude, the fame anxious infirmity, that
prompted thefe men to make fuch requefts,
in *later* and more *experienced* times, about
things at no great diftance ; prompt our firft
parent, with ftill greater force, to make the
like requeft on this *firft* promife? A promife,

[y] See Gen. xv. 8--xxiv. 14. Ex. iii. 11, 12. Judg. vi. 17.
37. 2 Kings xx. 8—11.

which,

which, poffibly, he might never live to fee accomplifhed.

In all this there appears to be nothing, but what is extremely natural; unlefs you would rather fuppofe, that God was fo gracious as to anticipate his wifhes. But, whether requefted or fpontaneoufly offered, here is, as it feems neceffary there fhould be, a very fignal miracle performed; and moft admirably adjufted to the tenour of the prophecy. God had faid, that " the feed of the woman fhould bruife the ferpent's head." In proof of what he had faid, he now devoted the ferpent to deftruction; ftripped him of all his pride and pre-eminence of form; and degraded him to the abject ftate of a reptile. This miraculous infliction plainly pointed out to what the promife tended; and exhibited a kind of vifible fecurity for the accomplifhment of the hopes it imparted. For when Adam, on that promife of victory over the ferpent, beheld him thus inftantly humbled and debafed; would he not readily admit this prefent, initial degradation of his enemy, as a fignificant prelude

lude to—would he not naturally efteem it, as a comfortable pledge of, his future and final overthrow? And muft he not joyfully conclude, that the virtue of the prophecy was intended to reach and benefit himfelf, when he faw it thus beginning to operate, as foon as it was communicated to him? Truly, one would be apt to think, that he broke out into the like grateful acclamation at this fight, as Simeon uttered at the fight of Chrift: "Lord, now letteft thou thy fervant depart in peace—for mine eyes have feen thy falvation²."

This promife then, confirmed and illuftrated by its attendant miracle, was excellently adapted to the wants and neceflities of fallen man; and communicated to him fuch hopes of falvation, as might encourage him to exercife a reafonable religion. But here it is to be obferved, that the religion of a *finner* muft be very different from that of an *innocent* man. And therefore we find, that there was now a change, and a remarkable change, made in the form of Adam's devo-

---

² Luke. ii. 29, 30.

tion

tion and worfhip, fuited to the change which
had happened in his circumftances: or, in
other words, that there was a new inftitution of religion eftablifhed. And this new
inftitution it concerns us particularly to look
into; becaufe it lies at the root, and runs
through all the branches, of the divine œconomy ; through all the difpenfations of religion from that to the prefent time.

It is clear from the words of the prophecy,
that fin was not to be *freely* forgiven ; but
required an atonement to be made for it:
that the ferpent could not be conquered, nor
the mifchiefs of the fall repaired, but by
" the fufferings of the woman's feed—" by
having " his heel bruifed." What this
phrafe of " bruifing the heel" might pre-
cifely mean, we have not at prefent fufficient
inftances in the *Hebrew* language to afcertain. In a kindred language however, that
is, the *Arabic* ; the root, from whence the
word בקע, viz. *heel*, is derived, fignifies
among other things, to " fuffer for fin—"
and alfo, to " die," or " fuffer death."

ª Vide Castell. Lexic. Hept. in radice בקע.

And

And if Adam underftood it in this fenfe; or
if God now declared to him (what was afterwards well known to his pofterity) that "without fhedding of blood there was no remif-
fion [b];" then we fee plainly the ufe and propriety of that inftitution, I mean *animal facrifice,* which we find eftablifhed at this time.
For if " Jefus Chrift—" moft emphatically " the feed of the woman—" was, in
the divine determination, " the lamb flain
from the foundation of the world [c];" what
could more aptly typify his death, than the
oblation of an innocent animal? And when
we read, that God cloathed our firft parents
with the fkins of thefe facrificed animals,
what are we to infer? that he meant only to
protect their bodies from the inclemency of
the weather? It feems far from being the
whole of the cafe.   The act is capable of a
higher meaning; and may alfo refer to the
fecurity of their fouls.   For in how fignificant, though emblematical, a manner, was
it adapted to reprefent to them—that this of

[b] Heb. ix. 22.
[c] Rev. xiii. 8.

facrifice

facrifice was the only method, by which their "tranfgreffion would be forgiven, and their fin be covered[d]?"

If you admit this interpretation, it plainly fhews, that facrifice, *animal* facrifice, was a kind of *facrament*; which, at the fame time that it fet forth the demerit of fin, carried in it a pledge of pardon and forgivenefs, through faith in the promifed Redeemer: and without which faith it was of no avail; as may eafily be deduced from the account we have of the facrifices of Cain and Abel.

But *Faith* was not the only condition of acceptance: *Obedience* was alfo required at their hands. For here it is evident, that as our firft parents were received into a new covenant, fo were they placed again in a new ftate of trial; and endowed with ftrength for farther fervices. What thefe fervices were to be, we may readily infer from the declaration of God in the text: " I will put enmity between thee and the woman; and between thy feed and her feed[e]." Now en-

[d] Pfal. xxxii. 1. See Hammond in loc.
[e] Gen. iii. 15.

mity

mityimplies an oppofition of will, inclination,
and intereft. And therefore, enmity to the
evil being muft infer a love and fidelity to the
good one [f]. The words then are fairly capable of this meaning—that, as the grand
apoftate would continually endeavour to fe-
duce them and their pofterity to fin; fo it
was their duty continually to endeavour, on
the other hand, to repel his temptations,
and keep themfelves ftedfaft in virtue; as
the only way of becoming at laft fit objects
of farther mercy. An enmity and victory
were both predicted: and, as they knew, to
their woe, that the *tempter's* firft conqueft
over *them*, confifted in his making them
finful, and expofing them to God's difpleafure; fo it muft needs appear, that their
reciprocal conqueft over *him*, muft be again
of a fimilar nature: that it muft confift
in becoming righteous and good: in main-
taining fuch an uniform practice of religion and virtue, as might finally reftore
them to the divine favour, and their ori-

[f].Rev. exam. Ibid. p. 62.

ginal

ginal tranquillity of mind.   And what elfe could they conclude from their reprieve? from the time that was allowed them after their fentence? but only, that it was to be a time of probation and difcipline; in which, though they might fuffer many things for a punifhment of their fin; they might yet exhibit daily proofs of their fidelity in the war againft " the feed of the ferpent;" and of their earneft concern to be reconciled to God by a fteady obfervance of his will and commands.

But to fupport them under the difficulties of this warfare, and to keep them fteady in this virtuous fervice, they had great need of fome *Encouragements*. This life afforded them but a melancholy profpect: For here they were irrecoverably doomed to labour, forrow, pain, and death. They muft therefore look to another ftate; of which the very delay of their fentence gave them no mean, no flight intimation. For furely they could never imagine, that

they were spared merely to undergo these
troubles; to contend with diseases; to fight
a tedious war with their enemy ; to raise
up children to succeed them in the same
train of sorrows; and then sink into dust
and oblivion. No. Their fairer hopes, me-
thinks, might be, especially when they knew,
that the war was at last to terminate in a
victory ; that they should reap some fruits,
some advantages from it : And since these
fruits and advantages were not to be obtained here, that they were reserved in
store to reward their patience and fidelity
hereafter [s].

And in these hopes they might be farther
confirmed by the words of the sentence
pronounced upon them.   For the sentence
adjudged that part of them only to *death*,
i. e. to *dust* or dissolution, which had been
formed out of the dust.   But that part
was the *body :* and therefore the *soul*, as an
immaterial, living principle, was not affected by it; but might still remain, and

[s] WINDER's H. of. Kn. vol. I. ch. ii. § 2.

continue

continue to exift in a feparate ftate, after the fentence had taken place [h]. In this feparate ftate then, our firft parents might rationally expect, if they perfevered in the ways of righteoufnefs, to enjoy at length fome comfortable bleffings; fome of thofe valuable bleffings they had loft: to enjoy fome part of their paradifaical happinefs; of that calm, ferene, and fpiritual happinefs, which they had formerly experienced, when they ftood partakers of the divine favour, and were approved by their own on fciences.

This expectation, then, of fuch great reward in a future ftate, was encouragement fufficient to keep them fteady in the uniform practice of virtue and religion. And upon the ftrength of this encouragement,

[h] What Adam's notion of a future ftate might really be, we know not: but to that part of the fentence paffed upon him—" Duft thou art, and unto duft fhalt thou return---" the Targums fubjoin thefe remarkable words: Attamen ex pulvere fufcitandus es, ut reddas judicium et rationem omnium quæ feceris, in die judicii magni. Vide in Gen. iii. 19.

fome

some of their posterity afterwards advanced to an eminent degree of piety and holiness. They opposed the immoralities of the antediluvian times; bore the scoffs and contradiction of sinners; withstood the temptations and allurements of the world; and finished a painful, exemplary course, in hopes of a blessed immortality. For they that could act in such manner, and give up the comforts of the present life, plainly declare, that they sought a better and nobler inheritance—" even an inheritance eternal in the heavens."

Allow this reasoning to be just; and it evidently appears, that the true religion—which is the point I would inculcate—has been always the *same* from the *fall* of Adam; subsisting ever on the *same* principles of *faith*, and leading men on to a virtuous *obedience*, in hopes of attaining *eternal happiness*.

And hence again we may, finally, perceive, how nearly an infidel came once to the *truth*, in the title of a book, which he

profes-

profeſſedly wrote againſt it.   For it is obvious, I preſume, from what has been ſaid,
that "Chriſtianity is" almoſt " as old as
the creation.".

Now to God, &c.   *Amen.*

SERMON V.

JUDE, ver. 14, 15.

And Enoch alſo, the ſeventh from Adam, pro-
pheſied of theſe, ſaying; " *Behold the Lord*
cometh with ten thouſands of his ſaints, to
execute judgement upon all, and to convince
all that are ungodly among them, of all their
ungodly deeds, which they have ungodly
committed, and of all their hard ſpeeches
which ungodly ſinners have ſpoken againſt
him."

WE have ſeen our firſt parents, after
their fall, admitted into a new covenant; eſtabliſhed on a ſpecial promiſe, and
confirmed by ſignificant rites. Theſe rites,
performed at ſtated times in the place appropriated to the purpoſe ; that is, on every

ſabbath

fabbath before the *fhechinah*[i]; were excellently adapted to preferve in their minds a
due fenfe of the mercies of that covenant;
and to render them attentive to the terms
and conditions, on which they were to enjoy the benefits of it. Nor is there any room
to doubt, but that our firft parents were careful to comply with thefe terms; and to teftify their gratitude for what God had done,
by their fteady performance of what he required [k].

It was not long, however, before they obferved the pernicious effects of their great
offence, in the contrary behaviour of fome
of their children. " Sin now began to
reign in their mortal bodies ; and they obeyed
it in the lufts thereof [l]." For Cain and his
defcendants, following the propenfities of
their corrupt inclinations, fell away, regardlefs of their duty, into all the abominations
of vice and immorality : " every generation,

[i] Winder's H. of Knowledge, vol. I. ch. ii. § 1. Taylor's
Sch. of Scr. Div. ch. xiv, &c.

[k] Vide R. Eliezer *Pirke*, c. xx.

[l] Rom. vi. 12.

one

one after another, not only imitating, but even furpaffing, the wickednefs of the former ᵐ."

In procefs of time, the pofterity of Seth, making alliances with the defcendants of Cain, became infected with the fame contagion; and at length degenerated fo far, that all fenfe of the true religion was entirely loft and extinguifhed among them.

Thus both the branches of Adam's family, the whole antediluvian race (a few only excepted) fell away from their allegiance to God; from the worfhip and fervice they were bound to pay him; and funk, as will hereafter appear, into grofs idolatry, fuperftition, and magic; and into a general licentioufnefs, and depravation of manners. For at this period, we are told, that "the wickednefs of man was great in the earth; and that every imagination of the thoughts of his heart was only evil continually ⁿ."

[ᵐ Joseph. Antiq. Jud. lib. I. c. ii. § 2. Eutych. Annal. p. 25.
ⁿ. Gen. vi. 25.

Having

Having taken this general view of the ftrange corruption of the antediluvian race; let us now look back, furvey in a more particular manner the foul fource from whence it fprung, and then trace it through the feveral gradations by which it rofe and increafed in the world. For, thefe things being known, we fhall be better able to difcover the propriety, reafonablenefs, and expediency of thofe extraordinary methods, which Providence made ufe of, time after time, to check its growth and retard its progrefs.

It is abundantly evident from the Scripture-account, that Cain was early infected with " an evil heart of unbelief° :" and therefore it is no wonder, that he fhould foon " depart from the living God." The firft act of worfhip he performed, was performed in hypocrify; which muft render it of courfe deteftable to him, " who pondereth the heart, and requireth truth in the inward parts ᴾ." And accordingly we read, that " the Lord had

° Heb. iii. 12.
ᴾ Pf. xli. 6.

refpect

respect unto Abel, and to his offering ;" becaufe it was brought in faith and fincerity: " but unto Cain, and to his offering, he had not refpect ⁹. "

This preference, which fhould have taught him the indifpenfable neceffity of inward ho- linefs ; and fhould have put him upon cor- recting and reforming his heart : this pre- ference, I fay, inftead of producing thefe fa- lutary effects, incited in his breaft ftill viler paffions, which urged him on to the blackeft deed. " He was thereupon, fays the text, very wroth ; and his countenance fell ʳ :" that is, he was ftrongly agitated with grief and anger ; vehemently tranfported with indigna- tion and revenge.

In this ftate of mind God kindly accofts him ; exhorts him to calm and moderate his refentment, and to refrain from the indul- gence of fuch criminal paffions. " Why is thy countenance fallen ˢ ? And why art thou fo wroth" with thy brother, when the fault

⁹ Gen. iv. 4, 5.
ʳ Ibid. ver. 5.
ˢ Ibid. ver. 6.

is entirely thine own? " If thou doeſt well, ſhalt thou not be accepted? and if thou doeſt not well, ſin," that is, the puniſhment of thy ſin, " lieth at the door ';" follows the act, and will inſtantly overtake thee. And here beware: for the appetite or deſire of a certain ſin now rageth in thy breaſt: " but" (as it is excellently expreſſed in an old Engliſh verſion) " let it be ſubdued unto thee; and ſee thou rule it ʰ." This is the reading of MATTHEWS's Bible ˣ; and CRANMER's is to the ſame ſenſe, though not quite ſo clear. But that defect is amply ſupplied, in the edition of 1585, by the following marginal note—" Sin doth provoke and ſtir thee to kill thy brother; take heed, and give no place to it; but reſiſt it, and be lord over it."

Adopt this tranſlation, which is ſufficiently exact, and ſupported by the *Targums* and

---

ᵗ Gen. iv. ver. 7.
ᵘ Ibid. ver. 7.
ˣ Printed in the year 1537.

ancient

ancient Verfions ᶻ ; and it manifeftly appears, how extremely folicitous the Lord was, that Cain fhould fupprefs the luft of revenge, and keep it from breaking out into fin. Nor is it lefs apparent how corrupt and depraved his heart muft be, who, notwithftanding this kind admonition and remonftrance, could yet perfift in his wicked defign, and imbrue his hands in his brother's blood. This innocent blood called for vengeance ; and it fpeedily overtook the murderer. For God pronounced him accurfed; banifhed him from the place where he then refided ; and expelled him from his own prefence ʸ : that is, in modern language, *excommunicated*, or, *cut him off* from the privilege of public worfhip.

ʸ The words which we now tranflate—" Unto thee fhall be his defire, and thou fhalt rule over him—" are thus paraphrafed in the *Jerufalem* Targum. .Verum in manum tuam tradidi poteſtatem concupifcentiæ malæ, tu autem dominabere ei. That of *Onkelos*, and of *B. Uziel* is to the fame purpofe. Arabic verfions Ad te fpectat moderatio ejus, &c. The propriety of this interpretation, refpecting the circumftances of the cafe, is well fupported by Dr. Jeffery in his Select Difcourfes, II. p. 53, &c. And the objections made to it from the anomaly of the language, taken in this fenfe, are anfwered by Ainfworth, &c. on the place.

ᶻ Gen. iv. 11—14.

A pu-

A punifhment fufficiently fore; and, as himfelf complains, hard to be borne. For it
was, in fhort, to caft him off as a reprobate;
to leave him, deftitute of grace, to the perverfe counfels of his own heart, to fill up
the meafure of his iniquities ; and, in the
event, to confign him over to utter deftruction [a].

This Cain plainly underftood ; and therefore was afraid, that " every one that fhould
find him, would immediately kill him [b]."
But God preferved him, as a monument of
the vengeance that awaits fin ; and kept him
in life, as a ftanding monition to the reft of
the fons of Adam; who might read in *his*
fate a very ufeful leffon to *themfelves*. For
hereby they muft needs be convinced, that
God took cognizance of human actions : that
no fin, however fecret, could efcape his notice : that every offence would be brought to
account, and meet with its condign punifhment : and confequently, that there was no
other way of avoiding mifery, and fecuring

[a] See GROTIUS, LE CLERC, and PATRICK in loc.
[b] Gen. iv. 14.

happi-

happinefs, than by a fincere attachment to
piety and goodnefs.—But we muft quit thefe
reflections, and follow Cain into the land of
banifhment.

Now, tinctured, as he was, with bad principles; and excluded from the eftablifhed
means of improvement; it is natural to infer, that, in this land, he became ftill more
depraved in his morals, and funk deeper into
vice and fenfuality [c]. And if we confider
likewife the effects of fenfuality, how apt it
is to debafe the mind, and to extinguifh the
evidence of things not feen; it is but too
probable, that his religious fentiments, if he
had any left, foon languifhed and fell into
decay; or at leaft degenerated into idle fuperftitions.

If you fuppofe this to be the cafe; and it
is by no means an unreafonable fuppofition;
then it clearly follows, that his feveral defcendants, committed to the guidance of
corrupt nature, without inftruction, and
without reftraint, muft needs deviate more

[c] See Jude, ver. 11. and the Com. thereon. Joseph. Ant. Jud.
lib. I. c. ii. § 2. Heidegger. Hift. Patriar. Exerc. V. § 45.

and

and more from the paths of truth and virtue; and, being at length enflaved to their unruly paffions, muft be carried on, as thofe paffions moved them, into every kind and degree of iniquity.

And now, as a *proof* of this charge, let it here be remarked, that, in the whole hiftory of the line of Cain, we meet with no inftance, no trace, no intimation, of any one virtuous, or truly religious action; but a great deal of the contrary. Inftruments of violence are found in their hands; and the harp and the pipe are heard in their feafts [d]: which plainly imply, that they gave themfelves up to fenfual enjoyments—which plainly imply, that they were luxurious, luftful, and debauched at home; and abroad, unjuft, rapacious and cruel.

In the midft of this corruption, however, they ftill entertained, we may well prefume, fome faint notion of a Deity. For this notion is fo connatural to the mind of man, that no people upon earth were fo far loft to the fenfe of things, as to be utterly devoid

---

[d] Gen. iv. 21, 22. Joseph. Ant. Jud. Lib. I. c. ii. § 2.

of

of it. But then, as the Cainites could have little or no knowledge of the fupreme, invifible Being, with whom they never had any intercourfe; fo it is extremely probable, that they addreffed their devotions, fuch as they were, to thofe vifible objects, with whofe appearance they were moft affected, and by whofe influence they were moft benefited. This, we are fure, was the cafe of the world in after-times; which is no fmall prefumption, that it was the cafe in the prefent. Some indeed have endeavoured to eftablifh this opinion on the authority of Scripture [c]: but, whether the Scripture countenance it or not, certain it is, the earlieft records of heathen antiquity fpeak fully to the point. For Sanchoniatho exprefly affirms, that " in a time of great drought Cain and his wife lifted up their hands, and prayed to the Sun; whom they looked upon

---

[c] Vide Targum ONKELOS et JONATH. BEN UZIEL, in Gen. iv. 26. MAIMON. de Idol. in Cap. i. et Notis. SELDEN de Diis Syr. Prolegom. Cap. iii. MARSHAM. Can. Chron. Sæc. iv.

as the fole god and fovereign of heaven [f] :"
and *they* might be alfo particularly induced
to deify and adore this fplendid luminary
from another motive; namely, as it carried
the neareft refemblance to that glorious
Shechinah, before which they had formerly
been ufed to celebrate the rites of divine
worfhip [g].

Soon after this, as the fame hiftory informs us, the like worfhip was extended by
their pofterity to the feveral parts of nature:
to the heavens, moon, and ftars; to fire, air,
and wind; to the earth, trees, and water;
to beafts, birds, and reptiles [h]. All thefe indeed

[f] Ἐκ τύτων τὰς γινομένας κληθῆναι ΓΕΝΟΣ κ) ΓΕΝΕΑΝ—αὐχμῶν δὲ
γινομένων, τὰς χεῖρας ὀρίζειν εἰς ὀρανὰς πρὸς τὸν ῞ΗΛΙΟΝ· τῦτον γάρ,
φησι, θεὸν ἰνόμιζον μόνον ἐρανῦ κύριον, ΒΕΕΛΣΑΜΗΝ καλῦντες. Apud
Eufeb. Præp. Evangel. lib. I. cap. x. p. 34. That Γένος and
Γινιὰ are Cain and his wife, Bifhop Cumberland has proved at
large, in his Remarks on Sanchoniatho, p. 219, &c.

[g] PATRICK's Com. Gen. iv. 16.

[h] Ἔχεις δὲ κ) ἐν τῇ Φοινιχικῇ θεολογίᾳ, ὡς ἄρα Φοινίκων οἱ πρῶτοι,
φυσικοὶ, ἥλιον κ) σελήνην κ) τὰς λοιπὲς πλανήτας ἀςέρας, κ) τὰ ςοιχεῖα
θεὸς μόνον ἐγίνωσκον, κ. τ. λ. Jam in Phœnicum etiam Theologia
reperias, qui principes apud illos naturalis fefe philofophiæ ftudio
dediderunt, eos folem pariter atque lunam, cæterafque ftellas in-
errantes, elementa præterea, quæque cum iis conjuncta funt,
deorum

deed are not diftinctly fpecified as fo many objects of their adoration : *moft* of them, however, are ; and *all*, I think, implied. For, when we are affured, that "they deified and adored the plants of the earth;" we can hardly doubt of their advancing the other, and far nobler, parts of the creation to the like honour[i].

In confequence of this worfhip, the arts of magic, forcery, and divination, were ftudied and practifed ; and fuperftitious, obfcene rites were inftituted and folemnized among them[k]. Thefe deteftable rites of their religion naturally inflamed their paffions ; and hurried them ftill farther into all the exceffes of outrage and violence, of licentioufnefs and debauchery[l], in civil life.

deorum in loco habuiffe. Iifdem porro mortales vetuftiffimos terræ germina dedicaffe, quibus divinitatem ipfi quoque cum adorationis cultu tribuebant.——Euseb. Præp. Evang. lib I. cap. ix. p. 28. cap. x. p. 34.

[i] Vide Heideg. Hift. Patr. Exercit. viii. De Theolog, Cainitarum, et Idololatria Antediluviana.

[k] Phil. Byel. apud Euseb. Præp. Ev. vol. I. c. x. p. 35. Athanas. de Incar. Verbi Dei. tom. I. p. 64.

[l] Gen. vi. 11—13.

I 2   Now,

Now, whilft the defcendants of Cain lived
in this impious and profligate manner; the
line of Seth went regularly on, under the
good conduct and tuition of Adam, in the
due obfervance of the duties of religion, and
the uniform practice of a holy life.   In the
third generation, in the days of Enos, we
meet with a fignal inftance of their zeal for
the honour and glory of God, and for the
prefervation and improvement of his worfhip
and fervice.   For " then they began to call
themfelves by the name of the Lord ᵐ;" that
is, the fervants and worfhipers of the true
God; in contradiftinction to the Cainites,
who had no regard or veneration for him.
This name, which they now affumed,
plainly intimates, that they devoted themfelves to a ftricter life of holinefs and virtue,
than they had led before; and that, for fear
of being " feduced by the errour of the
wicked," they prudently kept themfelves, as
God intended they fhould, from all commerce
or communication with the apoftate line. In
this ftate of feparation, diligent and atten-

ᵐ Gen. iv. 26.

                                    tive

tive to their vows and obligations, they
made, it fhould feem, great advances in
virtue and goodnefs ; and, for their extraordinary piety, were entitled the people or " fons
of God ⁿ."

How long they continued to improve
themfelves, or even to preferve the virtuous
attainments they had already made, is a
matter of fome uncertainty. Sure, however,
we are, that, in the fucceffion of few generations, they declined, and " fell from their
own ftedfaftnefs ;" yielded to the fuggeftions
of their fenfual appetites; and became foon
renowned for their enormous crimes ⁰.

This defection, great as it was, the Scripture accounts for in a very natural and eafy
manner. When both families " began to
multiply," and to extend themfelves ; they
approached, of courfe, nearer to each other.
Their vicinity foon drew them into mutual
converfation ; and that converfation into
clofer alliance. For when the " fons of
God," the pofterity of Seth, " faw the daugh-

ⁿ Gen. vi. 2.
⁰ Joseph. Antiq. Jud. lib. I. c. iii. § 1.

ters

ters of the men" of the other line; they were fo fmitten with their beauty, that, contrary to the charge of their pious anceftors, and probably to the command of God, " they took them wives of all which they chofe ᴘ;" that is, fuch, and perhaps fo many, as they liked to poffefs. The confequence of this interdicted affinity was plainly then, as it has always proved in fimilar cafes fince, ruinous to all piety. The line of Seth was hereby corrupted. For " the daughters of men turned away thefe fons of God from following him ;" led them to ferve other gods ; to affociate in all the abominations of idolatry, and all the impurities of a fenfual life.

This opinion is not only founded on the natural and experienced courfe of things; but feems to be confirmed by the very words of Scripture. For thefe, if I am not miftaken, were the *Nephilim*, the *apoftates*, mentioned Gen. vi. 4. " who kept not their firft eftate," but *fell off* from the fervice of God, and became *giants* in wickednefs, and *rebels*

ᴘ Gen. vi. 2.

againft

againſt heaven ꟼ. Their children, of the next generation, endowed with their ſtrength, and encouraged by their example, broke out into the ſame enormities; ˎand filled the world with impiety, idolatry, rapine, and violence. "Theſe mighty men," ſays the text, "were of old men of renown ʳ." A form of expreſſion, which clearly intimates, that their exploits and characters were conveyed down through ages by tradition; and might, at length, be inſerted in ſome ancient book, called "the book of Enoch," to which the Apoſtle refers.

In what period of the antediluvian age this apoſtacy happened, the Scripture does not expreſly determine. Data, however, it affords, by which we may ſettle it with ſome preciſion. At the twenty-ſecond ˎverſe of the ivth chapter of Geneſis we read—"And the ſiſter of Tubal Cain was Naamah:" A piece of information, which may appear, at firſt ſight, of little or no importance. But

---

ꟼ נפילים defectores, apoſtatæ, gigantes, rebelles, a נפל coecidit, defecit, irruit, &c.

ʳ Gen. vi. 4.

if

if we tranflate her *name* into our own language, it will inftantly throw an amazing light on the prefent fubject ; as it will aptly connect *this* verfe of the ivth with the *firft* of the vith chapter, where the caufe of the defection is particularly defcribed. For Naamah ' fignifies *fair* or *beautiful :* and when we are told, that the pofterity of Seth married the daughters of the other family, becaufe they were *fair ;* may we not reafonably conclude from this connected view of the paffages, that the facred hiftorian meant to inform us, that Naamah was the firft, the nobleft, and the moft . celebrated of all thofe beauties, with whom the alliance was made ?

If you allow this conclufion to be juft, then the opinion of the Arabian writers, who fuppofe the defection to have happened in the days of Jared ', will appear to ftand on good ground, and to be well fupported by the authority of Scripture.

' נעמה amœna, jucunda, pulchra.

' Vide ALMACIN. et PATRICID. apud HOTTINGER. Smeg. Orient. c. viii. p. 235. in voce *Jared.* HEIDEG. Hift. Patr. Exer. xi. p. 310.

But

But this is not the only thing, which the foregoing remark brings to our knowledge. It thews us likewife the reafon, why Mofes, in the genealogy of the line of Cain, ftopped at Lamech, the father of Naamah. He could properly proceed no farther : becaufe the diftinction was then at an end; as both the families became intermixed, and intimately blended with each other.

The fad effect of this unlawful mixture we have already feen, in that violent inundation of vice and impiety, which iffued from it, and which foon overflowed the world.

To account for this impiety in a more determinate manner, it may be of ufe to obferve, that Adam was ftill alive : and " becaufe the fentence," pronounced " againft" him for his " evil work," was not yet " executed" upon him; " therefore," it fhould feem, " the hearts of thefe fons of men were fully fet in them," both to think, and " to do evil ." The fentence deferred they might impioufly deride, as a vain and empty

ᵘ Eccl. viii. 11.

threat.

threat. And of the *predicted seed* they might
scoffingly say, " where is the promise of
his coming [x]?" These " hard speeches,"
which the prophecy of Enoch implies they
made, evidently amount to what St. Jude
calls, ver. 4. " denying the only Lord God,
and our Lord Jesus Christ:" evidently
amount, not only to a denial of the revealed
plan of redemption; but to a total disbelief
of an over-ruling providence, and a future
state—which Cain, it is said, disbelieved
before them [y]. When they had once brought
themselves to think, that either there was
no God; or that he was so regardless of
human affairs, as neither to reward the
good, nor punish the wicked; it is no
wonder, " they should thenceforth walk,"
without remorse, after their own ungodly
lusts; and give themselves over unto lasci-

---

[x] 2 Pet. iii. 4.

[y] The *Jerusalem* Targum, and that of Jonathan Ben Uziel,
introduce Cain conversing with his brother Abel in these words—
לית דין ולית דין וגו non est judicium, nec est judex; non
est seculum futurum, nec dabitur præmium bonum justis, nec
ultio sumetur de improbis, &c. Vide in Gen. iv. 8.

viousness,

vioufnefs, to work all uncleannefs with greedinefs [z]." For the reftraints of religion being now removed, there was nothing left to check or controul the perverfenefs of their nature.

If you admit this to be a true reprefentation of their moral ftate; and thus the Scripture feems to reprefent it; then fomething, 'tis plain, was neceffary to be done, as well to correct the erroneoufnefs of their principles, as to reform the depravity of their manners. At this time therefore, and with this view, a *fecond* revelation came feafonably in, exactly correfpondent to their neceffities and condition. For Enoch was commiffioned to preach the doctrine of a future ftate, and to declare the certainty of a future judgment.

In purfuance of this commiffion, he opened the profpect of another-life, and laid it before them in its different circumftances: he fhewed them what glorious rewards awaited the righteous, and what

dreadful

dreadful punifhments were referved for the wicked; " what tribulation and anguifh" fhould hereafter fall " upon every foul of man that doeth evil; and what honour, glory, and peace" fhould be the lot of him " that worketh good[a]." Thefe things he clearly laid before them[b]; that, knowing the encouragements and terrours of the Lord, they might be influenced thereby to return to him. And what can be imagined more influential? What could prevail, if this could not? Had it refted only on the bare credit of the preacher, a doctrine of this vaft importance would have juftly merited their moft ferious regard. But, that nothing might be wanting either to engage their attention, or to confirm their belief, God was pleafed to exert himfelf in an extraordinary and miraculous manner; and to atteft the truth of what his

[a] Rom. ii.9, 10.

[b] See Jude 14, 15; where the punifhment of the wicked plainly implies that there will be likewife a recompence to the righteous.

3

prophet

prophet had fpoken, by a proper, convincing fign. For what more proper, more convincing fign could they poffibly have in proof of fuch a doctrine; than to fee the prophet tranflated alive[c], and carried up, in a confpicuous manner before their eyes, into that very ftate, the exiftence and reality of which he had juft before revealed to them[d]?

Such doctrine, one would think, fupported by fuch evidence, would have borne down all oppofition, and fubjected the world to the authority of its dictates.

The doctrine itfelf was admirably calculated to correct thofe impious notions they maintained; and to make them fenfible, that God infpects the conduct of men in this world, and will recompenfe them hereafter as their works deferve. Its

[c] Gen. v. 24. Heb. xi. 5.

[d] See Targ B. Uziel, in Gen. v. 24. And hence Enoch was called Metatron, the perfon *removed on high*: from מטט and דם. This is at leaft as plaufible an account of the name, as any of the various ones already given.

attendant

attendant miracle, the tranflation of the prophet, was a vifible proof of his high regard for his faithful fervants; and a fure token of his firm determination to make them happy in a better ftate[e]. To Adam, if he was then alive, as the *Samaritan* account fuppofes, this remarkable event muft have been a lively and affecting inftance of what he might have enjoyed, had he kept his innocence; as well as an earneft of the promifed victory over *him*, who had robbed him of it[f]: And to his *fons*, if he was dead, as the *Hebrew* account declares him, it muft have afforded a feafonable and animating confolation under the depreffing fenfe of their own mortality: And to *all* it muft have fuggefted a forcible and cogent argument for repentance; as it carried a clear and comfortable intimation, that if they " walked with God," and overcame the finful inclinations of their nature, they fhould finally be reftored to the favour of

[e] Worthington's Effay on Hum. Redemption. ch. iii. § 6.
[f] Bp. Law's Theory of Rel. part ii. p. 60.

their

their Maker, and behold his prefence in blifs and immortality. And repentance, we might expect, would have accordingly; followed. But alas! we have an inftance now before us, that nothing is fo forcible, interefting, and perfuafive, but what the depravity and perverfenefs of man can with-ftand and reject. For this abandoned race, deaf to thefe awakening calls, obftinately continued their vicious courfe, and at laft perifhed in their wickednefs.

But, though " the word then preached did not profit them[g] ;" yet to *us* it remains of excellent fervice. It fhews us, that true religion was always the fame; and had always the fame end in view. Its whole defign has ever been to call men off from the practice of vice to ferve the living and true God; to make them virtuous in this life, that they may be happy in the other. This is apparent under every difpenfation; and more efpecially under the difpenfation of

[g] Heb. iv. 2.

the

the Gofpel: by which " we are made truly complete; being fully fupplied with all the things pertaining unto life and godlinefs [h]."

Having therefore fuch means of improvement in our hands, let us carefully make ufe of them. For if God punifhed the old world for defpifing the revelations delivered to them; how can we poffibly expect to " efcape, if we neglect fo great falvation [i]?" Let us ever remember, that the Gofpel is an inftitution peculiarly calculated for the advancement of piety and virtue : and let it effectually engage us, as it plainly teaches us, " to deny ungodlinefs and worldly lufts; and to live foberly, righteoufly, and godly in this prefent world; looking for that bleffed hope, and the glorious appearing of the great God, and our faviour Jefus Chrift [k]:"

[h] 2 Pet. i. 3.
[i] Heb. ii. 3.
[k] Tit. ii. 12, 13.

To

To whom, with the Father and the Holy Ghoſt, be aſcribed, as is moſt due, all honour and glory, might, majeſty, adoration and praiſe, both now and for evermore. *Amen.*

SERMON VI.

GEN. vi. 3.

And the Lord said, My spirit shall not always strive with man; for that he also is flesh: yet his days shall be an hundred and twenty years.

IN my last Discourse I laid before you a very ample account of the strange corruption of the antediluvian race: where I endeavoured to shew, from what bitter source it originally sprung; in what different forms it displayed itself; and by what growing advances it gained upon the world; till it be-

K 2 came

came at length fo univerfally prevalent, as to lay the Almighty under the fad neceffity of " deftroying man from the face of the earth [1]."

It is obferved by the author of the book of *Wifdom*, that " idolatry is the beginning, the caufe, and the end of all evil [m]." And this obfervation we have feen verified in the conduct and converfation of Cain and his defcendants. For no fooner did they forfake the true God, and engage in the worfhip of falfe deities ; no fooner did they begin to " efteem either fire, wind, or the fwift air, the circle of the ftars, the violent water, or the lights of heaven to be the gods that governed the world [n] ;" but, in confequence of the fervice they paid them ; in confequence of " the fecret ceremonies ufed, and the revellings of ftrange rites performed ;" they gradually fell into all the abominations of vice and immorality, and into all the ex-

[1] Gen. vi. 7.
[m] Ch. xiv. 27.
[n] Wifdom. xiii. 2.

ceffes

cesses of outrage and violence, both in public and private life.

In procefs of time, thefe impious principles and deteftable practices gained admittance into the other line: where they fpread and prevailed with fatal fuccefs, and with aggravated degrees of malignity. For, as the beft, when corrupted, become the worft; fo it is afferted of the pofterity of Seth, that " for the degree of zeal which they had formerly fhewn for virtue, they now fhewed by their actions a double degree of wickednefs[o]."

Such was then the ftate of the world. When " the Lord looked down from heaven upon the children of men, to fee if there were any that would underftand, and feek after God;" behold, he found that " they were all gone out of the way," that " they were altogether become abominable[p]." " For the wickednefs of man was great in the earth; and every imagina-

[o] JOSEPH. Ant. Jud. lib. I. cap. iii. § 1.
[p] Pfal. xiv. 3, 4.

K 3   tion

tion of the thoughts of his heart was only evil continually [a]."

But this progreffion of vice the great and righteous Governour of the world cannot be fuppofed to look upon with an eye of indifference. The perfection of his nature, the concern he maintained for the fecurity of religion, and the advancement of human happinefs, lead us to conclude, that he would rather interpofe, and kindly throw in the way of thefe profligates, as many checks, prohibitions and reftraints, as were confiftent with the freedom of moral agents. Nor is this conclufion deftitute of the fupport and countenance of Scripture. For the words of the text plainly imply, that " God *did* often ftrive with man ;" that he made ufe of various and powerful methods, as well to deter him from the commiffion of fin, as to keep him ftedfaft in the practice of virtue.

It has been already obferved, that " the *feed* of the woman was finally to deftroy the power and tyranny of fin and Satan, by

[a] Gen. vi. 5.

his

his steady attachment to truth and righteoufnefs. Now this confideration muft naturally
infpire all wife and thinking parents with a
deep concern and zealous care, that their
children might be inftructed in the principles
of religion, and trained up in the paths of virtue.
And fuch care they muft ftill be the more
anxious to employ, becaufe they perceived,
that all their hopes, both for themfelves and
their pofterity, depended upon this rectitude
or uprightnefs of difpofition ; without which
it was impoffible that any of them could be
the *promifed feed*, who was to reftore again
the human race to its original purity and
perfection [r].

Here then was laid an excellent foundation for the inftruction and improvement of
the rifing generations. And the fuperftruc-
ture erected upon it was equally good. For,
as they advanced in life, thofe documents of
virtue, which they had received in their
youth, were ftill renewed from time to time;
being conftantly inculcated and enforced on
their minds by the enjoined obfervance of

[r] Rev. exam. vol. I. differt. ix. p. 155.

the

the eftablifhed rites of worfhip. For every
fabbath, which they celebrated in its weekly
return—every facrifice which they offered—
and every public act of religion they performed, ferved to convince them of the ma-
lignant and deftructive nature of fin, as well
as to imprefs them with a due fenfe of the
neceffity of holinefs.

By thefe means, which were all *ftanding*
means of inftruction, the inhabitants of the
old world, had they not been greatly wanting to themfelves, might have made a truly
laudable proficiency in the knowledge and
practice of religion. Negligent, however, as
they were; when they became degenerate,
and had foolifhly deviated from the path of
duty, the *occafional* tranfactions of the times,
the *incidental* difplays of divine government,
fupplied them with powerful and awakening
motives to recal them to repentance and a
better life.

Their great Father continued among them,
above *nine hundred* years, a living monument
both of the juftice and mercy of God: a
living monument of his extreme hatred and

abhor-

abhorrence of fin; as well as of his tender
love, and compaffionate regard for the
finner:—and therefore, a monument, one
would conceive, that muft daily fuggeft
fuch arguments to their thoughts, as could
hardly fail either to awe, or to allure them,
into ftricter obedience.

And the fame moral inftructions were alfo
conveyed by *other* occurrences. For, as the
punifhment of Cain exhibited to the world a
woful proof of the dire effects of vice and
impenitence; fo was the exaltation of Enoch
into heaven, one of the nobleft incitements,
that can well be imagined, to the confcien‑
tious practice of piety and goodnefs.

Add to thefe, as operating to the like pur‑
pofes, the frequent exhortations and admoni‑
tions of their prophets; and more efpecially
that tremendous punifhment denounced againft
them by the prophet Enoch: who, fore‑
feeing it would be executed by a *deluge*, impofed
on his fon the name of Methufelah, by way
of fign and confirmation of it. For the word,
Methufelah, imports, that, when the perfon
fo called *is dead*, there fhall enfue an *inunda‑*

tion

tion of waters[s]. And so exactly did the event correspond with his name, that in the very year he died, the earth was overwhelmed by the deluge.

Now, after the delivery of this alarming prophecy, transmitted to us by St. Jude; such was the patience and long-suffering of God, that they had no less than *eight hundred* years allowed them, to reflect on their condition; to repent of their wickedness; and to amend their ways. And in the course of this time they were moreover solicited, encouraged, and admonished to the due performance of these necessary duties, by the repeated instructions and good examples of those holy men, who were sent among them as " preachers of righteousness[t]."

---

[s] Ita Enoch propheta summus, cum prophetico spiritu prævidisset cladem illam (diluvium) filii mortem statim subsecuturam, vocavit illum מתושלח Methuselah. Quo nomine significabat statim *illo mortuo* futuram *emissionem* sive *aquarum inundationem* in perniciem mundi totius. BOCHART. Phaleg. lib. II. c. xiii. p. 100.

[t] Of whom, it should seem, there were no less than eight. For St. Peter calls Noah ὄγδοον δικαιοσύνης κήρυκα. 2 Pet. ii. 5.

5

But,

But, notwithſtanding theſe methods of mercy and monition, which God in his goodneſs employed for their amendment; yet, when he came again, at the end of this period, to take cognizance of what they had done, he found them immerſed ſtill deeper in vice and ſenſuality; " being then really nothing but fleſh [u];" that is, entirely devoted to ſenſual gratifications, and conſtantly purſuing " the works of the fleſh."

Now, the works of the fleſh have in all ages been ever the ſame. And were therefore in the *antediluvian*, as in the *apoſtolical* times, moſt probably theſe: " Adultery, fornication, uncleanneſs, laſcivioufneſs, idolatry, witchcraft, hatred, variance, emulations, wrath, ſtrife, ſeditions, hereſies, envyings, murders, drunkenneſs, revellings, and ſuch like [x]"— vices that called, eſpecially when grown to ſuch enormous height, for a ſignal and ſpeedy vengeance.

Accordingly the Lord (having before adminiſtered proper conſolation to his few,

[u] Gen. vi. 3.
[x] Gal. v. 19—21.

faithful

faithful fervants) ʸ now pofitively affured
this impious generation, that his fpirit would
neither

ʸ That they fhould receive fuch confolations was manifeftly neceffary for their encouragement in well-doing: and that they did
receive them is plainly implied in that prophecy of Lamech,
which he delivered at his fon's birth, " This fame fhall comfort
us concerning our work and toil (labour) of our hands, becaufe
of the ground which the Lord hath curfed." Gen. v. 29. The
fenfe of which, varioufly interpreted, paffage feems to me to be,
in fhort, as follows—" This fame Noah fhall bring us full and
ample comfort for all the pains and difficulties we have under-
gone in fupporting the caufe of truth and virtue. Through him
it will appear, that our labour is not in vain in the Lord. For
when God comes to punifh the ungodly, and to deftroy the
world by a deluge, (fee note ˢ p. 138) he will give us, in the
perfon of this man, a fignal inftance of his tender regard for the
good and righteous. For he will conduct him fafely through that
perilous fcene, and land him fecurely on a new world, which we
may look upon as an earneft of that future inheritance, which is
referved for us, who have walked in the fame paths of righteoufnefs." Comp. Heb. xi. 7.—To make out this meaning, I conceive that the words—" Our work, and labour of our hands—"
fhould be taken here, as they are often elfewhere, in a *moral*, and
not in a *natural*, fenfe—and that the " curfe" here mentioned
has no reference to that denounced at the *fall*, but means the
deftruction to which the earth was devoted, and which was accomplifhed by the deluge; as will appear to any one, who com-
pares Gen. ch. v. 29, with ch. viii. 21.
    Lud. Cappellus, in his Comment on the place, confiders it
nearly in the fame light. Senfus ergo fimpliciffimus eft: Gaudebit
                                                    terra.

neither ftrive, nor his patience bear any
longer with them, than for the fpace of an
hundred and *twenty* years : and that he was
then determined, if his vengeance was not
averted by their amendment, to deftroy them
by an utter excifion from the earth.

But this denunciation, like the former,
inftead of producing its defired effect, and
bringing them back to penitence and piety,
ferved only, by the perverfenefs of their incorrigible difpofitions, to harden them the
more in their wickednefs : infomuch, that
when God, towards the clofe of this momentous period, infpected their conduct the third
time ; he faw they had filled up the meafure
of their iniquities ; and were completely
fitted for that approaching deftruction, to
which they had been juftly devoted. Such,
I fay, was their ftate, when God beheld
them the *third* time. For it is a point
worthy of obfervation, that in the account

terra, exultabunt pii homines, quum Dei juftitiam in impios homines vindictam fub hoc meo filio futuram, novamque mundi
faciem per eum exorituram, in nova hominum fobole ex eo ema-
natura, confpecturi funt.

here

here given of the growing degeneracy of mankind, there are *three* gradations diftinctly fpecified; each of them in fucceffion furpaffing the other, and appearing in blacker colours. At the *third* verfe of this chapter[2], they are defcribed as " *carnal*—" fulfilling the lufts of the flefh. At verfe the *fifth*, they are reprefented as *fixed* and *rooted* in their vices—" their wickednefs was GREAT; and every imagination of the thoughts of their hearts was only evil CONTINUALLY." This is ftrong painting: and yet, at the *eleventh* verfe, it is ftill greatly heightened. For there, the *ground* is faid to be *tainted* with their fins; and to *groan* under the weight of their iniquities—" The earth was *corrupt* before God, and the earth was *filled* with violence[a]." Now, by CORRUPTION the moft approved of the Jewifh writers generally underftand *idolatry*, and the tranfgreffion of what we call the *firft* table of the law: and by VIOLENCE is plainly meant every kind of *inhumanity* and *injuftice*, or the total breach of

---

[2] Gen. vi.

[a] Vide MUNSTER, et VETABL. &c. in loc.

the

the *second* table: and therefore, from both expreffions taken together, we may juftly conclude, that the human race was, at this time, fo far loft to all fenfe of religion and morality, as to be entirely regardlefs of every duty, which they owed either to God or man [b].

Noah indeed preferved his integrity; and ftood, amidft the general corruption, a fingular example of true piety and virtue. This diftinguifhed behaviour entitled him there-

[b] If the foregoing account of the moral ftate of the antediluvian world be admitted as tolerably juft, then the *Præcepta Noachidarum*, or the precepts delivered to the fons of *Noah*, will appear to ftand on good ground; as being well adapted to the condition of the times, and feemingly founded on the reafon of things. For if mankind, forgetful of God, were then prone and given to *idolatry*; how neceffary was it, that they fhould be ftrongly prohibited that practice by a pofitive law, Ift. De cultu extraneo; and brought back to a due fenfe of the divine *majefty* by a IId. De maledictione nominis fanctiffimi, vel numinis? If they were *violent*, *cruel*, and *revengeful*, how proper was it to reftrain their paffions by a IIId. law, De effufione fanguinis? If *luftful* and *debauched*, by a IVth. De non revelanda turpitudine? If *rapacious* and *fraudulent*, by a Vth. De furto ac rapina? And, if regardlefs of *juftice* and *equity*, by a VIth. De judiciis, feu regimine forenfi ac obedientia civili? &c. Thefe laws, thus applied, derive weight from the ftate of the world; and at the fame time throw light upon it.

fore

fore to diftinguifhed favour: which he accordingly experienced in the wonderful prefervation of himfelf and family. " For the
Lord knoweth" as well " how to deliver the
godly from diftrefs and danger, as to re-
ferve the unrighteous to the day of judgment, to be punifhed [c]" with a feverity pro-
portioned to their guilt and wickednefs. And
this day was now haftening towards all them
that dwelt on the earth. For, fince they had
all, by their degeneracy, utterly defeated
the defigns of Providence; and could by no
means be brought to anfwer the proper ends
of their creation : nay, fince they lived indeed to fuch purpofes, as were directly contrary to thofe ends, and wholly deftructive
of them—lived only to rebellion and difobedience to their maker; and to their own mutual mifery and deftruction [d]: fince this, I
fay, was the cafe with them; it was certainly high time, that God, in mercy as
well as juftice, fhould put a fpeedy period
to their exiftence—as being the only way to

[c] 2 Pet. ii. 9.
[d] Revelation Exam. vol. I. diff. ix. p. 163.

clear

clear the world of that corruption, which, through the courfe of fo many centuries, he had laboured in vain to correct and remedy. Accordingly therefore, when " the long-fuffering," with which he waited in the days of Noah; and " the preparation of the ark[e]," the laft effort of his mercy, could have no effect upon them; he then fuffered his indignation to arife; gave a loofe to his vengeance ; and delivered them all, at once, to death—" bringing in the FLOOD upon the world of the ungodly[f]."

Should it now be afked, " Why did God make ufe of this, rather than any other method?" The anfwer, I think, is eafy : Becaufe it was the propereft, and the moft conducive to the purpofes of his providence; the moft adequate to his grand defign. Ido-latry, it is evident, could not be extirpated ; piety and virtue could not be reftored ; till that *incorrigible* race was utterly deftroyed, and a better introduced in its ftead.

[e] 1 Pet. iii. 20.
[f] 2 Pet. ii. 5.

" But

" But the deſtruction of thoſe impenitents might have been accompliſhed, you will ſay, by various *other* means, as well as by a *deluge*." Doubtleſs it might. But what if *their* de-ſtruction was not the whole intent? What if God had farther ends in view, reſpecting thoſe who ſurvived? How will matters ſtand then? It is no unreaſonable ſuppoſition, this. For, as the ſons of Noah had converſed a long time with that corrupt and ſinful gene-ration; and were perhaps, ſome of them, cloſely connected with the apoſtate line; it is more than probable, that they were in ſome degree infected with the idolatrous principles, and vicious practices of the age. What thoſe *practices* were, we have already ſeen §; and ſtand in need of no farther information about them. But with regard to the *principles* of the times, as they are the grand key to this diſpenſation, it may be of uſe to conſider them here again.

There is a certain prediction concerning the inhabitants of the old world, attributed to Enoch, and preſerved by Tertullian, which

§ Page 159.

ſets

fets forth their religious tenets in a clear light. Now, from this prediction it appears, that they were fo deeply immerfed in fuper-ftition and errour, as to deify all nature :—— " that all the elements, the whole furniture " of the univerfe, things in heaven, things " on earth, and things under the earth, were " feverally perverted by them to the vile pur- " pofes of idolatry ; and fet up as objects of " divine worfhip [h] ;" In a word, it appears; that they confecrated and adored almoft every thing, except Him, who alone is truly ado- rable : and Him they were in no wife dif- pofed to ferve.

Now, if the fons of Noah were in any degree tinctured with thefe notions ; and in- clined to follow fuch examples [i] ; they were

fo

[h] Antecefferat Enoch prædicens, omnia elementa, omnem mundi cenfum, quæ cælo, quæ mari, quæ terra continentur, in idololatriam verfuros dæmonas, et fpiritus defertorum angelorum, ut pro Deo adverfus Dominum confecrarentur, &c. TERTULL. de Idololatria § iv.

[i] Cham, filius Noë, fuperftitionibus illis et facrilegis artibus infectus fuit. CASSIAN. apud KIRCHER. Obelifc. Pamph. lib. I. c. i.

so far the less likely to preserve and maintain the true religion in its genuine state and purity. And had they continued in that disposition, the design of Providence might have been utterly frustrated; as " the work of the Lord must have failed in their hands."

The security of religion therefore, and the interest of morality, plainly required, that the present manifestation should carry something in its nature and form, equally adapted to convince them of the erroneousness of these principles, as to deter them from the practice of the forementioned vices. And what, I beseech you, could better answer these several purposes, than the very transaction we are now considering?

If it really was, as it seems to have been, the prevailing opinion of those times, that the *world* was self-existent, independent and eternal; then the Almighty, to assure and convince them that he both made and go-

Lord Barrington in his Exposition of 1 Pet. iii. 17—22, makes it extremely probable, that all Noah's sons, &c. were disobedient and irreligious till they entered into the ark—where they reformed and became penitent. Miscell. Sacra, vol. iii. p. 199. note ʳ ed. 1, 70.

verned

verned it, did, as it were, unmake it again: inverting its laws, and abolifhing its order.

As we have fome reafon to believe, that that *water* and *air* were their chief divinities; fo we accordingly find, that God made *them* the chief inftruments of his wrath and ven-geance.

As the *earth* was perhaps efteemed the mother of the gods—of thofe animal, rep-tile, and vegetable deities, that fubfifted on its furface; fo the Lord deftroyed the *earth* and its products, together with every ani-mal; fuch only excepted as were preferved in the ark for the reftoration of the fpecies.

And left the fons of Noah fhould attri-bute this terrible execution to the agency and power of fome falfe deity [k], God foretels them that himfelf would do it, and fpecifies the time and manner of it. " After feven days, behold I —" not any of your imagi-nary deities—but " I JEHOVAH do bring a flood of waters upon the earth, to deftroy all flefh, wherein is the breath of life, from

k See If. xlviii. 5.

under

under heaven. Every thing that is in the earth fhall die[1]."

This marvellous event therefore, the avowed work and operation of God, did not only ferve to enforce on their minds a ftrong conviction of his fupremacy and power; but carried alfo a fenfible confutation of all thofe impious and fatal opinions, on which the ancient idolatry was founded. It clearly fhewed, that JEHOVAH had no rival: and fince to him only belonged glory, dominion, and power; fo to him only fhould be given worfhip, adoration, and praife.

I have no occafion to obferve, for it is extremely vifible, with what irrefiftible force this punifhment of the wicked, by the very things wherein they had finned, muft operate on the minds of Noah's family, who were eye-witneffes of it: how it muft awaken their attention; fill them with the moft awful ideas of God's holinefs and purity; convince them of his unchangeable averfion to fin, and abhorrence of its abettors; and confequently deter them from the like provocations. For

[1] Gen. vi. 17.—vii. 4. 10.

whatever

whatever prefumption the long-fuffering of
God might have nourifhed before in the
breafts of daring and hardened finners; yet
now, the vain hopes of efcaping his vengeance, otherwife than by repentance and
a good life, muft all neceffarily vanifh—
muft all die, abforbed and buried in the
common wreck of the fhattered world.

If we limit the defign of Providence in
this tremendous event, to the bare deftruction of thofe who perifhed; I can fee no
good reafon, I own, why the Deity fhould
ufe fuch a complicated method, and fum-
mon all the elements, to put it in execution;
" fince, without thefe, they might have
fallen down with one blaft, being perfecuted
of vengeance, and fcattered abroad with the
breath of his power[m]:" much lefs can I account, why the earth was demolifhed, and
every living creature deftroyed. But, if we
view this tranfaction in the light it is here
placed; and confider it as moreover intended
to *correct* the *errours* of them that were preferved; then every circumftance will carry

[m] Wifd. xi. 20.

L 4   with

with it its ufe and beauty; and the whole will appear to have been ordered and conducted according to the rules of confummate wifdom.

Having thus feen the intent and propriety of this difpenfation, with regard to the ftate and condition of the world, at the time when Providence brought it to pafs; it now only remains, that we draw from it the proper inference, refpecting ourfelves and our own times. For fuch is the nature of thofe difpenfations, which are recorded in Scripture; and fo widely are they extended by that unity of defign, which runs through them; that the events which happened in the earlieft ages " are profitable for correction and inftruction in righteoufnefs[n]," even to the lateft generations. The things that happened to the *antediluvians*, carried their influence down through the FLOOD, and are meant to operate to the CONFLAGRATION. " They happened to *them* for enfamples; and are written for *our* admonition[o]:" " to the

[n] 2 Tim. iii. 16.
[o] 1 Cor. x. 11.

intent,

intent, that we fhould not luft after evil things, as they formerly lufted [p] :—" to the intent, that we might learn wifdom at their expence; nor prefume to follow them in the ways of difobedience; " confidering the end," the difaftrous end, " of their conver-fation [q]."

Irreligion and idolatry, profanenefs and immorality are in their own nature, and according to the eftablifhed order of things, injurious and detrimental to man : and this confideration ought in reafon to put us upon our guard againft them. But if neither the dictates of reafon, the admonitions of revelation, nor the inconveniences we feel in a wrong courfe, can prevail upon us to correct our mifdoings; then God himfelf, as gover-nour of the world, is obliged to take us into his own hands; and to urge us with feverer and more extraordinary inflictions. How " fearful a thing it is to fall into the hands of the living God [r]," the inftance before us is

[p] 1 Cor. x. 6.
[q] Heb. xiii. 7.
[r] Heb. x. 31.

an alarming proof! But if " they, who defpifed" the *antediluvian* prophets, and the lefs
perfect " law" that was then given, " died
without mercy ;" " of how much forer punifhment, fuppofe ye, fhall he be thought
worthy, who hath trodden under foot the
Son of God—and hath counted the blood of
the covenant, wherewith he was fanctified,
an unholy thing—and hath done defpite
unto the fpirit of grace¹ ?"

That our hearts therefore may be preferved
under an awful impreffion of the divine judgements, let us frequently meditate on thofe
difplays of them, which are fet before us in
the holy Scriptures. And when we reflect,
that the " old world," for the wickednefs
of its inhabitants, " perifhed by *water* ;"
let us alfo remember, that " the prefent
world is kept in ftore, referved unto *fire*
againft the day of judgment, and the per-
dition of ungodly men¹."

And fince the *one* element will as certainly
diffolve " the world that now is," as ever the

¹ Heb. x. 28, 29.
¹ 2 Pet. iii. 6, 7.

other

other deluged " the world that then was;"
let us endeavour, like Noah, by keeping the
ways of truth and piety, to fecure the pro-
tection and favour of God; that, when the
time comes, we may finally, like him, be
fafely guarded, conducted and admitted into
" that new heaven and new earth—" into
that glorious and eternal kingdom, which
God hath prepared for them that love him;
and " in which dwelleth righteoufnefs,"
peace, joy and happinefs for ever-more.

Now to God the Father, &c. *Amen.*

S E R-

SERMON VII.

GEN. xi. ver. 4—8.

*And they said, Go to, let us build us a city, and
a tower, whose top may reach unto heaven;
and let us make us a name, lest we be scattered
abroad upon the face of the whole earth.*

*And the Lord came down to see the city and
the tower, which the children of men builded.*

*And the Lord said, Behold, the people is one,
and they have all one language; and this
they begin to do: and now nothing will be
restrained from them, which they have imagined to do.*

*Go to, let us go down, and there confound their
language, that they may not understand one
another's speech.*

So

So the Lord fcattered them abroad from thence
upon the face of all the earth: and they left
off to build the city.

WEN-Noah was landed on the prefent earth, and happily faw his
piety rewarded with fuch an amazing inftance of divine favour; there is no room to
doubt, but that he made religion his chief
concern, and zealoufly propagated it among
his pofterity. Thofe religious notions and
cuftoms*, which his fons and their defcendants carried down along with them into the
feveral countries in which they fettled, are
inconteftable proofs of his care and diligence
in this refpect.

But, notwithftanding the feverity of God
in punifhing the fins of the *old* world, and
the induftry of Noah in providing for the
inftruction of the *new*; yet mankind in a
fhort time degenerated again; and funk apace
towards the fame ftate of depravation, that

---

* Such as the notions of *expiation* by *facrifice*; of a *Mediator*
between *God* and *men*, &c; the cuftom of *facrificing*; and the
obfervation of the *fabbath*, or keeping *holy* the *feventh* day, &c.

we have reprefented them to have been in before the flood.

Now, that the world fhould degenerate fo faft, and forget fo foon the firft principles of true religion, is what feems, in the opinion of a noble author, to be utterly incredible. But his opinion of things would have been very different, had he read the Scripture, as he ought to have done, with lefs prejudice, and with more attention. For then he would have found it fo far from being " impoffible, for *any* man in his fenfes to believe, that a tradition, derived from God himfelf, fhould be loft, in the courfe of fo few generations, amongft the greateft part of mankind ; or, that polytheifm and idolatry fhould be eftablifhed on the ruins of it in the days of Serug, before thofe of Abraham, and fo foon after the deluge [x]—" that, on the contrary, *every* man in his fenfes, who confiders the tendencies and operations of things, muft neceffarily conclude from the account which the facred hiftorian has given us, that fuch corruptions would take place;

[x] Lord Bolingbroke's Works, vol. IV. Effay II. p. 20.

and,

and, unlefs prevented by fome extraordinary providence, be likely to extirpate the knowledge and worfhip of the true God from off the face of the whole earth.

It fhall therefore be my bufinefs in this Difcourfe, to explain, in the

Firft place, how thefe corruptions came to be introduced; or, in other words, how idolatry and wickednefs came to fpread and prevail in the world fo very foon after the deluge.

And, when they did prevail, to fhew, in the

Second place, how excellently well the miracle of the text, the confufion of languages, was adapted to check their increafe and progrefs.

When the deluge had retired, and the ground was become capable of frefh cultivation, God, for the encouragement of Noah, to proceed with alacrity in that neceffary work, declared—that, notwithftanding the future provocations of men, he was fully determined, never to deftroy the earth again, in the manner he had now done. But, as

there

there appeared then no evil in the world,
Noah perhaps might wonder, whence thofe
future provocations could arife; or what
could poffibly give occafion to them. Hence
therefore the declaration, at the fame time
that it brought him the affurance he wanted,
led him to the knowledge of the point he
fought. For thus faid the Lord—" I will
not again curfe the ground any more for
man's fake; though the imagination of man's
heart is evil from his YOUTH[y]." Now here,
when the *firft* claufe, " I will not again
curfe the ground," conveyed to Noah the
neceffary confolation; for what other purpofe, but for his information concerning the
introduction of evil, could the *latter* claufe
be added? And what elfe, in due conftruction
of language, could he reafonably underftand
by it, but that, though iniquity had not
fprung forth, yet God faw the latent feeds
of it lurking in the heart of one of his fons?
or rather, as it fhould feem by the turn of

[y] Gen. vii. 21.

the expreſſion, lurking in the heart of his *youngeſt* ſon, Ham [z].

As this ſenſe of the paſſage ſtands ſupported by the grammatical conſtruction, ſo is it confirmed by the event that followed. For we advance but a little way farther in the courſe of this hiſtory, before we diſcover a ſtrange perverſeneſs in the conduct of Ham: before we diſcover thoſe ſeeds of iniquity, which had hitherto lain dormant in his heart, burſting out at once into a ſhameful irreverence towards his father, and horrid impiety againſt God: irreverence to his father, in openly expoſing and deriding his nakedneſs [a]—impiety againſt God, by his taking occaſion from thence, as the Jewiſh writers interpret the action, to make the promiſe of the Meſſiah a ſubject of ridicule.

This was a crime of an heinous nature—as it evidently aroſe from a ſpirit of infidelity; tended to defeat the purpoſe of Providence; and alſo to deſtroy the hopes of the world. It was therefore a crime that

[z] Gen. ix. 24.
[a] Ibid. 22.

deſerved

deferved to be feverely punifhed. And accordingly God, having obviated the mifchiefs of it by a repetition of the promife to
Shem and Japheth, paffed upon Ham a
judgment fuitable to his profanenefs and impiety. He cut him off from the bleffing he
had defpifed ; and devoted his pofterity to
the grievous curfe of being " fervants of
fervants to their brethren [b]."

When Ham and his pofterity found themfelves under this malediction, and clearly deferted of God ; it is natural to conclude, that
they, in their turn, deferted him ; and totally renounced his religion and fervice : It
is natural to conclude, that in their fubfequent feparation from the reft of their brethren, who were now become odious to them,
they chofe for themfelves *new* gods, as their
guides and protectors in their *new* fettlement. They fettled, it fhould feem, firft
in Arabia ; commonly ftiled in Scripture,
" *the Eaft*." But where-ever they fettled,
they carried with them a fenfe of the curfe :
and that fenfe would naturally prompt them

[b] Gen. ix. 25---27.

M 2

to

to provide againſt it, as well as they could. The beſt proviſion they could perhaps think of, might be the exerciſe of arms: to which therefore, it is to be ſuppoſed, they would apply themſelves in a ſpecial manner. And hence they might ſoon become, as the hiſtory tells us they did become, " mighty ones in the earth ᶜ." Conſcious of their own ſtrength, and elated perhaps with the appearance of ſecurity, they might think now of reverſing the doom ; and inſtead of ſubmitting to be ſubjeꝗ to their brethren, might arrogantly attempt to bring their brethren into ſubjeꝗion to themſelves.

Thus one would reaſon on the principles of nature. And in exaꝗ conformity to this train of reaſoning, Moſes aſſures us, that they aꝗually " made a journey," that is, a warlike expedition, " from the Eaſt ᵈ ;" paſſed over the Euphrates; and violently ſeized on " the land of Shinar," which was part of the

ᶜ Gen. x. 8.

ᵈ Gen. xi. 2. where the word נסע ſignifies not only to *jour-*
ney, but to *journey* with an *hoſtile intent.* See DAUBUZ on the
Revel. ch. xvii. 5.

inheritance

inheritance of the fons of Shem. The inhabitants of this land they foon fubdued: and
then, in the true fpirit of policy, built cities
or forts at convenient diftances, to awe, and
keep them in proper fubjection. " From
hence they went out into Affyria^e;" made
there the like conqueft; and built cities with
the like intent—to fecure the fidelity and
obedience of the vanquifhed^f.

This was a deep-laid fcheme; excellently
calculated to fupport their tyranny; and
therefore worthy of the hiftorian's notice,
however it may have efcaped the notice of his
readers. The author of this fcheme (planned,
by the bye, as an introduction chiefly to a
ftill more daring one) was Nimrod, the

---

^e Gen. x. 11. See the *marginal* reading; the Targ. of ONKE-
LOS, and of JON. B. UZIEL; BOCHART. Phaleg lib. iv. c. xii.
p. 259, &c. Others, following the reading of the text, maintain
that Ahur built Nineveh, and not Nimrod.

^f If we fuppofe Ninus to be the fame with Nimrod, the main
lines of this account, however diftorted, may yet be traced in the
hiftory of Ctefias, copied by Diodorus Siculus, Biblioth. Hiftor.
lib. ii. in principio.

M 3   grandfon

grandfon of Ham; whom the Scripture ftiles in our verfion, " a mighty hunter *before* the Lord [g];" but fome of the ancient interpreters of Scripture, " a mighty rebel *againft* the Lord [h]."

That he was indeed a " rebel," his very *name* implies [i]: and that his rebellion confifted principally in idolatry, is the general fuffrage of all antiquity. That he conveyed his idolatrous principles and practices into every place, where he carried his arms, is not only probable from the early cuftom, which obtained in the world, of obliging the conquered nations to embrace the religion of the conquerors; but is inconteftably

[g] Gen. x. 9.

[h] The Jerufalem Targum, as alfo that of Jon. B. Uziel, tranflates the words thus—Ipfe (Nimrod) incepit effe potens in peccato, et ad rebellandum coram Domino in terra. Vide in Gen, x. 8. Ita lxx, Γίγας ἐναντίον κυρίε.

[i] The name נמרד Nimrod comes from מרד rebellavit, and was given him by his enemies, the Aſſyrians, who were defcended from Shem. His prior name, among his own people, was probably בעל or בל, Baal or Bel; and that of his city בית בל Beth-Bel—to both which names refpectively there feems to be a keen and clofe allufion in the fubfequent words בלל and בבל, Gen, xi. 9.

certain

certain from the traces we find, and the accounts we read of him, in ancient authors.
It is exprefly faid, that he taught the Chal-
deans, Perfians, and Affyrians the worfhip
of FIRE [k]; and, that he introduced among
them the ufe and exercife of *magical* arts—for
which he was highly celebrated by the
MAGI. A plain proof how very faft, and
extenfively wide, his idolatrous inftitutions
prevailed in the world.

Now, as thefe practices and opinions prevailed, the true religion muft of courfe decline: and more efpecially in thofe regions
that were fubject to the dominion of this infidel tyrant. But thofe were chiefly the regions inhabited by the defcendants of Shem:
which leads us to account, in a very eafy
manner, for that hitherto unaccountable
phænomenon, "The early corruption of this
facred line; even in its pureft and moft
facred branch." For it is not improbable,
but this zealous idolater might, as the Jerufalem Targumift declares he did, make a

---

[k] CLEMENT. Recognit. lib. I. § xxx. CLEMENT. Homil. IX.
§ iii, iv. &c. Chron. Alexand. et EUTYCH. Annal.

decree

decree among the people, " that they fhould every-where renounce the religion of Shem, and embrace his own inftitutions [1]."

But Nimrod's project did not terminate here. He had ftill farther and more perni- cious views. What he had gained by his fword, and introduced by his power, he de- figned to maintain, confirm and perpetuate. His intention, in fhort, was, to form an uni- verfal empire; and to fettle and eftablifh his religion and government among all people. In purfuance of this defign, when he had finifhed his conquefts (for fuch is the natural order of things, and therefore the real order of the hiftory) he fixed his eyes on Babel; which, as it " was the *beginning*," he de- termined now to make alfo the *capital*, " of his kingdom [m]." Accordingly he enlarged and improved it, as a fit feat for the civil

---

[1] ‏ויאמר להן, רחוקו וגו‏. Et dixit eis, " Recedite a religione Sem, et adhærete ad inftituta Nimrod." Vide in Gen. x. 9.

[m] Gen. x. 10. See alfo CTESIAS. ap. Diod. Sicul. ubi fupra. Whofe chief errour is, that he miftook Nineveh for Babel or Babylon.

magiftrate;

magiſtrate; and therein eſtabliſhed a *civil government*. He likewiſe built a tower in it, " whoſe top (not *might reach*, as we interpolate, but) *was conſecrated*, to the heavens [n];" that is, to the heavenly bodies, and particularly to the SUN; and ſo provided for the ſupport of *religion*. That this tower was intended for religious uſe, the altar on its top is a plain indication. And though the reaſon aſſigned for its *pyramidal* form, as being a proper repreſentation of the *ſpiring* nature of flame or fire, may perhaps be the refinement of later ages; yet, it clearly ſhews that, in the opinion of thoſe ages, it was originally built for a temple of the SUN [o], whoſe ſymbol is *fire*, that very element, which the builder of this tower firſt taught

---

[n] Gen. xi. 4.

[o] HERODOTUS obſerves (Lib. I. c. 181, 183.) that the tower of Babylon was ſacred to BEL, i. e. to the SUN. See p. 114. note [f]. And that ſacrifices were offered to him on the great altar in the upper ſtory. The pyramids of Egypt, built by this very people, I mean the deſcendants of Ham, were deſigned for the ſame purpoſe; viz. for *temples*, as well as *ſepulchres*. Whence that of the poet, Votaque Pyramidum celſas ſolvuntur ad aras. See more in TENISON of Idolatry, ch. iv. p. 42, &c.

the

the nations to worſhip; and now intended they ſhould worſhip for ever.

Such was his grand project. And in order to bring his people the more readily to embrace this project, he artfully told them—that it was the only way " they could make themſelves a *name* [r];" the only way they could advance themſelves to dignity and renown; and maintain their ſuperiority over the reſt of the world—that, if they broke this league and union, and divided into ſeparate parties, they would fall into the ſnare that was laid for them [q]; would be eaſily vanquiſhed in that ſtate of diſperſion; and ſo, being made ſlaves to their brethren, would become an ignoble and *nameleſs* race.

[r] Gen. xi. 4. *Faciamus nobis* שם *nomen*; famam, celebritatem. Sic, Gen. vi. 4. *Illi heroes a ſæculo* אנשי השם *viri nominis*; nobiles, celebres. Job xxx. 8. *Filii* בלי שם *abſque nomine*; nullius nominis, ignobiles. SCHINDLER. Lexic. in radice שמה.

[q] For Joſephus ſays, Πϱοσέθεσαν δὲ τῷ παϱακύειν τῆς τῦ Θεῦ γνώμης, κ. τ. λ. " that to their diſobedience to the divine will, they added the ſuſpicion, that they were therefore ordered to ſend out ſeparate colonies, that, being divided aſunder, they might the more eaſily be oppreſſed." Antiq. Jud. lib. I. c. iv. § 1.

This

This, it feems, worked on their minds, and engaged them all in that bold undertaking[r]; which, had it not been interrupted by heaven, would certainly have been accomplifhed in a fhort time. For when they had once made this beginning, " there was nothing," humanly fpeaking, (as they were all of one language and one mind) " that could reftrain them from doing whatever they farther imagined to do[s]." They were a ftrong and warlike people; and, having already acquired great conquefts, would foon have brought other nations (ignorant of arms, and intent only on the cultivation of the earth) fubject to their authority and power : and all thefe nations, thus fubdued, they would eafily have incorporated into one

---

[r] Here it may be neceffary to apprize the reader, that I do not think Nimrod's people, viz. the defcendants of Ham, to be the *only* people engaged in this attempt: *many* of the *other* lines, and efpecially of the line of Shem, whom he had lately conquered, probably joined themfelves to him; admiring his fortune, ftate, and magnificence. But the *principal agents* were his own people.

[s] Gen. xi. 6.

general

general empire, by that ftrongeft band of union, the general eftablifhment of the fame *civil* and *religious* inftitutions.

Now, had this defign taken place, and been effectually carried into execution ; the whole purpofe of Providence, with regard to the world, would have been utterly croffed and defeated. For the union of mankind under one monarchy would, of courfe, have prevented their difperfion ; at leaft for a confiderable time : Nor would it then have proceeded in that orderly manner, in which God had directed it to be carried on. In the mean while, the eftablifhment of *idolatry* by *law* would have foon fuppreffed, and at length extinguifhed, the *true religion.* And then, impiety and immorality of every kind (already, doubtlefs, but too rife among them) would have continually increafed, and extended their contagion : and this concerted univerfal empire would neceffarily have become one horrid fcene of univerfal wickednefs [t].

[t] Revel. examined, &c. vol. II. differt. iii. p. 99, &c.

When

When the adjuftment of things, not only pointed, but had begun to operate to this deftructive end; it is furely no more than what reafon leads us to expect, that God, in compaffion to mankind, as well as in vindication of his own authority, fhould gracioufly exert his power, and employ fuch means as his wifdom fhould direct, to defeat fo ruinous a project. Agreeably therefore to this expectation, the Lord is reprefented as coming down from heaven " to fee the *city* and the *tower*—" to infpect the fcheme of *religion* and *government*—" which the children of men," thefe daring infidels, " had planned and erected." And finding it fo contrary to the real intereft and happinefs of mankind, he immediately enters into this refolution :—" Go to, let us go down, and there confound their language, that they may not underftand one another's fpeech. So the Lord fcattered them abroad from thence," fays the text, " upon the face of all the earth : and they left off to build the city ᵘ." And by what means he effected their

ᵛ Gen. xi. 7, 8.

difperfion,

difperfion, is more particularly explained in the following verfe:—" Therefore is the name of the city called *Babel*," (viz. *confu-fion*) " becaufe the Lord did there *confound* the language of all the earth: and from thence did the Lord fcatter them abroad on the face of all the earth[x]:" that is, when God, by the confufion of their language, had divided them into diftinct tribes; the natural confequence was, that thofe tribes, feparating from each other, formed themfelves into fo many diftinct nations; and finally fettled in diftinct parts of the world[y].

And here, it is worth our while to obferve, in the

Second place, How apt an inftance this is, as well of the wifdom, as of the power of God: where we fee it fo amazingly fitted in every refpect to the circumftances of things, and the proceedings of this people: fitted to defeat and overthrow their fcheme—fitted to convince them of their folly and madnefs in concerting it—and equally fitted to de-

[x] Gen. ix. 9.
[y] Hestiæus apud Euseb. Pr. Ev. lib. ix. cap. 15.

liver

liver the world from the mifchiefs intended by it.

As their fcheme was planned, in defiance of heaven, to keep them clofe and united together, in order the better to obviate the curfe that was denounced againft them; what can we conceive more effectually adapted, to render them fenfible of the abfurdity of their attempt, than this ftrange confufion of their language?—whereby the Almighty difunited them again; and fo reduced them to that divided ftate, which muft neceffarily expofe them to the whole weight of the malediction? And that this was effected by the hand of God they muft needs perceive from the nature of the tranfaction. For as their language (to fpeak at the loweft) could be confounded only, by dividing it into feveral dialects; and giving their organs a new, inftantaneous ply, diverfly adapted to the different inflections, tones, and modifications of thofe feveral dialects [z]; fo the actual

---

[z] Various, I know, are the fentiments of the learned on this fubject. Moft of them, however, admit—that the language of thefe

actual introduction of such confusion must evidently be the result of divine power: a power which shewed them, in this instance as in many others, how easy it was for him, " to make the devices of the people of none effect, and bring to nought the counsels of princes[i]."

And as they united together, not only for their own defence, but also with a view of reducing the posterity of Shem and Japheth under the power and dominion of their sole monarchy—in consequence of which idolatry and wickedness must have increased among them; what surer method could Providence contrive, to free the world from the tyranny of Nimrod; to restore it back to

---

these builders was certainly *confounded*. And as the degree of confusion here specified, was sufficient to answer the end proposed; so, that it was in reality no greater, the *radical affinity*, still subsisting between the several *oriental* languages, seems to me to be a plain proof. Consult Is. CASAUB. in Adversariis, De *Linguarum Confusione*. Many are of opinion, that *new* languages were now introduced. But surely there is a great deal of difference between *forming new* languages (of which the Scripture says not a word) and *confounding that* which was before in use.

[a] Pf. xxxiii. 10.

5   its

its primeval divifions; and to hinder its
being corrupted in any higher degree from
that quarter, than this which he now employed? For by thus confounding the language of Nimrod and all his adherents, and
thereby dividing them into feparate, enfeebled
parties; God did not only open a way for
the conquered nations to affert their liberty,
and migrate according to the patriarchal
appointment; but he likewife cut off, ina
great meafure, all farther connection, intercourfe, and communication between *them*
and this wicked people; and even between
the feveral divifions of this very people themfelves: which muft neceffarily reftrain the
overflowings of iniquity, by dividing the
current, and reducing it into narrower
bounds.

But this is not all. For the judgment we
are now confidering, however fevere, was
mercifully calculated as well to improve this
wretched people, as to blefs and benefit the
reft of the world. In confequence of the
confufion, they divided, of courfe, into fo

many diftinct and different focieties, as there were different languages fpoken among them. Now, as thefe feveral focieties (feparating, I apprehend, under a divine impulfe, and therefore according to the divine defignation) would form themfelves, whenever they fettled, into diftinct governments, under their feveral heads; fo thefe feveral governments muft neceffarily contribute, in a very eminent degree, to the reftraint of vice, and the advancement of virtue. For, being conftitutionally obliged, each of them, to provide for the general good; they muft needs take care, that the conduct and behaviour of every individual fhould confpire to the welfare and happinefs of the whole. But the welfare of every fociety depends, in a fpecial manner, on the peace and harmony, on the courage and fidelity, and on the induftry, temperance, and frugality, which reign among thofe who compofe it. And therefore the members of fuch newformed ftates muft, and we fuppofe did, zealoufly cultivate, and diligently exert

7

thefe

thefe neceffary virtues for their own advantage.

Add to this, that the very jealoufies and
emulations which muft unavoidably arife between ftate and ftate ; the neceffity of defend-
ing themfelves one againft another ; and the
ambition of equalling or excelling each other:
Thefe muft keep them conftantly on their
guard, and attentive to the ftricteft difcipline [b].—And as they were, on the one hand,
forcible means to with-hold them from every
thing bafe and injurious ; fo were they, on
the other, as powerful incentives to great,
noble, and praife-worthy actions. And whatever, be it remembered, was gained hereby
to the account of virtue, was fo much more
than could poffibly have been obtained, had
the world continued, as was now projected,
under the loofe adminiftration of one general empire.

But this divifion of nations carried with
it another advantage ; and became fubfer-

[b] BURNETT's B. Lect. vol. II. p. 131. 8vo.

vient

vient to a ftill higher end. It laid the foundation for a more natural, and more equal
difpenfation of things.   For, under this circumftance, Providence could diftribute both
rewards and punifhments, in feparate and
exact proportions, according to the deferts of
every ftate.   If any ftate became fignally
virtuous above its neighbours; God might
blefs it with fignal favours, without its neighbours partaking of the benefit : or, if it unhappily funk into vice and wickednefs, there
was now no need of any immediate correction from above ; but one people might be
raifed to correct and punifh the faults of another, without the deftruction of either.   And
if any people, regardlefs of thefe flighter inflictions, fhould continue ftill incorrigibly
wicked, God might fafely cut them off,
without any danger of hurting the reft.
Nay, their excifion would be attended with
this falutary effect, that it would ferve as a
warning and caution to others, not to offend
l y the like crimes, for fear they fhould fall
under the like punifhment.   And all this,
                                        furely,

furely, muft be no fmall check to the feducing influence of bad examples, and the deftructive contagion of vice.

Having thus traced the rife and progrefs of idolatry and wickednefs in the
firft ages after the flood : And having
alfo explained how wifely and properly the
prefent difpenfation, the confufion of languages, and the difperfion of nations, was
calculated to reftrain this growing impiety ; and to preferve the knowledge of
God in the world ; I have only one reflection to make ; and that reflection is
this—that we fhould never defpair of the
final fuccefs, and firm eftablifhment of true
religion. It has been indeed often oppreffed ; and it may be fo again. But as
it is the religion of God, God, we may
depend, will protect and fupport it. However unfavourable the circumftances of
things may, at times, appear ; yet the marvellous wifdom of Him, who has the government of the world in his hands, and
who is fo vifibly concerned in the caufe

of

of this religion, will make " all things work together at laft" for its real " good" and advantage. If we look, at the time here commemorated, to the city of Babel, and' the plains of Shinar ; if we reflect on the decree which was then made, " that people fhould forfake the God of Shem, and caft off his religion and wor-fhip ;" the profpect, it muft be owned, is fad and difmal. But when we purfue the manifeftations of Providence, and confider the effects of his fubfequent operations ; what comfort muft it afford us to find again at a future period—that from this very *place*, and from thefe very *plains*, there iffued forth another decree, ftrictly com-manding " all people, nations, and languages, to honour the God of the defcendants of Shem ; and to confefs that He alone is the living God, and ftedfaft for ever ; and his kingdom that which fhall not be de-ftroyed ? [d]."

c See note (') p. 168.
d Dan. vi. 25, 26, ch. ii. 29.

O Lord,

O Lord, how manifold are thy works! and how adorable art thou in all thy doings, O King of Saints! To Thee therefore, with the Son and Holy Ghoſt, be aſcribed, as is moſt due, all honour and glory, &c. *Amen.*

SERMON VIII.

GEN. xii. 1—3.

*And the Lord said unto Abram, Get thee out
of thy country, and from thy kindred, and
from thy father's house, unto a land that
I will shew thee.*

*And I will make of thee a great nation, and
I will bless thee, and make thy name great;
and thou shalt be a blessing.*

*And I will bless them that bless thee, and curse
him that curseth thee: and in thee shall all
families of the earth be blessed.*

THOUGH the last-mentioned dispen-
sation—the confusion of languages,
and the dispersion of nations consequent
thereupon—gave some check to the progress
of vice and idolatry; yet is it evident, from

the

the accounts we have of the fucceeding ages, that it did not entirely ftop it. The depravation had been, alas! fo warmly foftered, and had gained, as we have feen, fuch growth and vigour, under the government of Nimrod, that it ftill furvived this fignal judgment; and, fpreading itfelf with the fpreading nations, foon prevailed over the whole world. For when the family of Shem, who had peculiar motives to attach them to God, are known to have deviated very early ᵉ into the worfhip and fervice of falfe deities; what elfe can we think of the reft of the nations, who manifeftly enjoyed much fewer advantages, but, that they accordingly funk into groffer idolatries?

When mankind, thus univerfally immerfed in idolatry, had loft the knowledge of God and his religion; how neceffary was it for their real happinefs, that fome new meafures fhould be employed, to bring them back to the recognition of his fovereignty, and the obfervance of his pure worfhip!

ᵉ In about 400 years after the flood, for which we have accounted in the laft difcourfe, p. 167.

But

But to reftore at once the true religion, and to preferve it in any degree of purity, among a world of people fo thoroughly depraved, would certainly have been a difficult, if not indeed an impracticable tafk. To facilitate therefore, and finally to fecure this neceffary point, God, in wifdom as well as kindnefs, called forth Abraham from his country and kindred, and made him the father of a new race and better generation: which was to be kept fequeftered from the reft of the nations: and trained up in the true knowledge and worfhip of Himfelf, and in the true faith of that fundamental principle of revealed religion, and powerful motive to virtuous obedience—the promife of a Redeemer.

Now Abraham was fixed upon, not from any fondnefs or partial affection, but becaufe he was a perfon of eminent character, and endowed with proper qualifications for the purpofe: one who had already given fufficient teftimony of his averfion to idolatry, and of his firm attachment to the God of heaven. For he had boldly maintained againft his own country-men, "that there was

but

but one God, the creator of the univerfe:
and that the other gods," whom they adored,—the fun, moon and ftars—" were only
inftruments in his hands: and if they contributed any thing to the happinefs of men,
that each of them afforded it by *his* appointment; and not by their *own* power [f].   And,
in defence of this doctrine, he had been, if
we may believe Maimonides, in imminent
danger of lofing his life [g].

As he was therefore a perfon well difpofed
towards God, himfelf; fo God foreknew,
that he would take care " to command his
children, and his houfhold after him, to
obferve and keep the way of the Lord [h]:"
and thereby approve himfelf an agent fit,
in every refpect, to be intrufted with the
conduct of that grand defign, which he was
chofen to guide and carry forwards.

But, though God made choice of Abraham
and his pofterity for the guardians of his

[f] Joseph. Antiq. Jud. lib. i. c. vii. § i.

[g] Mor. Nevoch. p. iii. c. xxix.   Vide Hotting. Smeg.
Orient. c. viii. § 19.

[h] Gen. xviii. 19.

true

true religion ; and confequently favoured them with peculiar privileges; yet is it by no means to be fuppofed, that he dropt his regard for the reft of the world, and had no farther concern for other people. The difpenfation was meant for the general good; for the common benefit of all mankind. For the text exprefly informs us, that by and from the call of Abraham, "all the families of the earth were to derive a bleffing." And it was no fmall part of this bleffing, that God, having appointed him and the fucceeding patriarchs to be the public vouchers of his being and providence, fent them out to bear his name before the nations ; to correct the errours they had unhappily imbibed; and to inftruct them in the ways of truth and righteoufnefs.

In confeqnence therefore of this appointment, and in purfuance of this gracious defign, we meet thefe holy men in the moft renowned and confpicuous places—in Chaldea, Canaan, and Egypt, the fofter-lands and nurferies of idolatry—we meet them, I fay, in thefe places, proclaiming and an-
nouncing

nouncing the unity of the Deity; afferting
his fupremacy againft all oppofition[i]; raif-
ing altars to the honour of his majefty[k];
and invoking him, in their folemn acts,
under the diftinguifhed character of " the
moft high God, the creator of heaven and
earth[l]."

Add to thefe, the frequent conferences
they are faid to have held with the priefts of
the nations among whom they fojourned;
and the conclufive arguments they are re-
ported to have brought in confutation of their
vain opinions[m]; and what can you conceive
better adapted, either to reform the ignorance of thofe nations, or to confirm the faith
of their own people? For as thefe conferences,
in which they difplayed a vaft fuperiority of
knowledge and wifdom, could not fail of
correcting, in fome degree, the popular errours and fuperftitions of the times; and of

[i] Joseph. Ant. Jud. et Maim. Mor. Nev. ubi fupra.

[k] Gen. xii. 7, 8.—xiii. 18.—xxvi. 25.—xxviii. 18, 19.—
xxxiii. 20.—xxxv. 7.

[l] Gen. xiv. 22. Heb. קנה שמים וארץ LXX. Ὃς ἔκτισε τὸν
ὐρανὸν κỳ τὴν γὴν. Vide *Lud. de Dieu* in loc.

[m] Vide Joseph. Maim. Hottinger, ubi fupra.

bringing

bringing thofe, with whom they converfed, to a jufter notion of God and his providence ; fo the conftant practice they ufed, of fetting up altars, where-ever they came, for the worfhip of the true God, was not only an exemplary proof of their own high fenfe of the divine majefty, and their continual dependance upon him; but alfo a noble and excellent method to teach and encourage their children and families to " fet the Lord ever before them, and in all their ways to acknowledge Him."

It is alfo to be obferved, that thefe pious patriarchs were highly favoured in all their migrations; and eminently diftinguifhed among the neighbouring princes. Even " kings were reproved for their fakes." And as thefe kings were acquainted with their prophetic character, and defired their prayers and interceffion with God[n]; fo the relief they obtained, in confequence of that interceffion, muft needs difpofe both them and their fubjects, to liften for the future with more attention to thofe fpiritual exhortations,

[n] Gen. xii. 17.—xx. 7.

counfels,

counfels and inftructions, which thefe holy men of God moft probably joined to the other inftances of their kindnefs.

Nor fhould it here be forgotten, that their numerous tribes of " men-fervants and maid-fervants," whether received as prefents, or purchafed with money, became in the event, by the care they took of their education and conduct, juft fo many profelytes, gained over to the true religion.

So early did the promife, " that in Abraham and his pofterity the feveral nations of the earth fhould be bleffed," begin to operate in the world : and fo comprehen-five was it, as to take in all ranks and de-grees among them ; and efpecially thofe of the loweft rank ; who perhaps then, as in the days of the Gofpel, were of all others the moft fincere, and the moft open to convic-tion.   And with regard to thefe menial fer-vants, as they were commanded, " though ftrangers," to be circumcifed ; and accord-ingly partook, with the Abrahamic feed, of the rite of circumcifion ° ; we may juftly, I

° Gen. xvii. 12, 13.

think,

I think, look upon them, as a kind of " firſt-fruits of the Gentiles ;" who carried in their admiſſion a manifeſt token, that; notwith-ſtanding the peculiarity then eſtabliſhed, all the Gentiles would be adopted at laſt, and ſhare the benefits of the divine covenant.

In a ſcheme of ſuch conſequence, evi-dently calculated for the common good, but attended in the execution with great dif-ficulties, it is natural to expect, that the hand of Omnipotence would be often exerted for the ſupport of its ſeveral parts. Indeed, the patriarchal age was altogether an age of miracles—which every eye, that views the circumſtances under which they were wrought, may eaſily diſcover the propriety of; and which therefore require no diſtinct or particular explanation. Some of theſe miracles manifeſtly tended to comfort and ſuſtain the patriarchs in their troubles ; and others to animate and ſpur them on in their great and arduous undertakings. But they all conſpired to render them powerful, illu-ſtrious and eminent : And that power and eminence, to which they were advanced, ferved to promote the general defign, and to forward the fcheme of Providence. For, as the intercourfe and converfation of the patriarchs brought the true, genuine religion to the knowledge of the nations; fo did their profperity and marvellous fuccefles recommend it likewife to their practice. For fince all the people among whom they fojourned, were every where attentive to the concerns of this world, and eagerly ambitious of temporal grandeur; it was but natural for them, when they obferved the profperity of the worfhipers of Jehovah, to make inquiry—what God he was, that could confer fuch bleflings; and what kind of fervices could procure and afcertain them: it was but natural for them to worfhip him too after the like manner, in expectation of receiving the like rewards.

Nor is this only a fpecious furmife of what might poffibly be, but rather a plain and fimple narration of what really was, the cafe. For feveral of the Eaftern nations appear to have adopted the patriarchal rites; and to have reformed their religion to, what they

they thought, the patriarchal purity. In proof of what is faid, let it here be remarked, that as hiftory informs us, of Abraham's converfing on the fubject of religion with the moft learned Egyptians; and of his being highly efteemed and honoured by them [p]; fo we have reafon to conclude from the fame hiftory, that they derived, among other religious inftitutes, the rite of circumcifion, which they practifed, from him. But fhould this be doubted, certain however we are—that the Magians, Sabians, Perfians and Indians, all gloried in him, as the great reformer of their religion [q]. And of the Perfians it is recorded in particular, that they adhered fo ftrictly to this reformed religion, as to keep clear of the moft grofs idolatry for ages and ages after. Nor is this any more, than what might reafonably be expected from other people, as well as from the inhabitants of Perfia. For whatever improvements Abraham introduced into the religion

[p] JoſEPH. Ant. Jud. lib. I. c. viii. § 2.

[q] HYDE De Rel. Vet. Perf. c. ii. iii. PRIDEAUX's Connect. p. I. b. iv. an. 486.

of

of the feveral nations; thefe, we may fuppofe, the reft of the patriarchs, wherever
they came, were folicitous to cultivate, promote, and confirm, as far as their influence
extended.

But the care which the great Father of the
nniverfe thus gracioufly employed for the re-
formation and amendment of the world at
large, was now to be more efpecially directed
and applied to the welfare and fecurity of
his peculiar people. The chofen branch of
Abraham's family was at this time increaf-
ing very faft. And as they were to be kept,
for the prefervation of their religion, in a
ftate feparate from all other nations; fo it
became neceflary, that a fuitable place fhould
be provided for them, where they might
commodioufly and fecurely live by themfelves. But, fince the world around them
was already inhabited, it is hard to conceive
where they could live fo fequeftered, unlefs
they were removed into fome defolate country; which yet, would have been utterly
inconfiftent with, and entirely fubverfive of,
the principal defign of their feparation. For

as

as they were feparated not fo much for
their own fake, as for the fake of the whole
world; for the conveyance and propagation
of the true religion; it was therefore neceffary, for the benefit of the world, that they
fhould be feen, known, and obferved; and
that they fhould be converfed with likewife,
in fome diftant manner, by the feveral people
around them. Now all this manifeftly tends
to increafe the difficulty. For to be totally
feparated from, and yet, at the fame time,
perpetually converfant with, other people; is
what appears, according to human eftima-
tion, abfolutely impracticable. "But what
is impoffible with man, is very poffible with
God." And here we cannot but admire his
wifdom, who found out, and evacuated a
land for them; I mean that of Gofhen; in
every refpect fuitable to the purpofe: A land,
where they might live diftinct by themfelves, and yet daily converfe with the moft
celebrated nation then upon earth: A land
lately deferted by the *fhepherd kings* and their
fubjects; and therefore the moft fitly adapted

for

for the reception of *shepherds* again [r]. Nor can we less admire his *goodness*, who, when he had " spied out this land for them," was pleased to detach " from his country and kindred" another person of eminent qualities and great piety; and to send him— " even Joseph, who was sold to be a bond-servant [s]—" as a kind of ambassador before them, to procure an interest for their settlement in it.

Now a slave in a strange country must appear to human view a very unpromising instrument of success in a matter of such importance. But the lower his condition was at first, the better it served to illustrate the interposals of divine Providence in the several stages of his advancement afterwards. For the hand of God is visible in every step; and his wonders enter into almost every

---

[r] See BRYANT's Observations on the ancient History of Egypt, &c. p. 140, &c. Art. " Of the Shepherds in Egypt, and the Land of Goshen," and the other Articles connected therewith. See particularly p. 159. And LE CLERC's Com. on Gen. xlvi. 34. only what he says of the Egyptian should be transferred to the Arabian shepherds.

[s] Psal. cv. 17.

transaction.

tranfaction. Thefe wonders performed in favour of Jofeph, are too numerous to be recited, and too obvious to be explained. This only need. we remark concerning them, that in whatever degree they promoted his particular and perfonal intereft ; in the very fame degree they contributed alfo to advance the general defign of his miffion ; to open the way for a more favourable reception of his brethren and their families, and for their more commodious fettlement, whenever they came.

When God had thus, by the mediation of Jofeph, provided for the fettlement of the children of Ifrael ; he then introduced them into the land of Egypt under all the advantages, with which they could poffibly wifh to be introduced. Their relation to Jofeph, who was univerfally efteemed, recommended them to the favour of the king and his fubjects. In confequence of this favour, they were placed in a large and fertile diftrict ; where they multiplied, and grew, and gathered ftrength ; and yet, by their very occupation, were ftill kept a feparate people.

Here

Here they lived after their own manner; and not only enjoyed the free exercise of their religion themselves, but had also many and frequent opportunities of imparting something of it to others around them. For it is very apparent from the Mosaic history, that the Hebrews were never held in such detestation or abhorrence by the Egyptians, but that they would freely converse, though " they might not eat bread, with them[t]."

In these conversations, then, it could not be, but that a people so signally supported by the Lord, would be continually extolling the excellency of his majesty—rehearsing the wonders of his various dispensations—and so infusing into the minds of the Egyptians noble ideas of his being and providence— the fureft foundation of virtuous improvement.

What effects the irruption of the Cusean shepherds, and their long tyrannical dominion over the land of Egypt, had produced before on the religion of its inhabitants, we cannot precisely determine. But as we know

[t] Gen. xliii. 32.

they

they were grofs idolaters, and brought with
them all the rites and inftitutions of Zabiani-
ifm, together with the worfhip of fire; it
is certain they could not improve, but muft
rather debafe, the religious fentiments of that
people ᵘ;—who, yet, muft become ftill more
perverted in their morals, by the continual
exertions of thofe hoftile paffions, which
they were daily provoked to exercife in oppofition to their cruel oppreffors. For a ftate
of perpetual war and confufion is a ftate of
perpetual wickednefs and immorality.

And if the confufed and oppreffed ftate of
the Egyptians tended thus, for a length of
time, to efface the truth, and diminifh the
power of religion among them; what can
you imagine better adapted to reftore the
practice of piety and virtue, than the marvellous exaltation of Jofeph? Being adopted
into the order, and placed at the head, of
the priefthood; his gratitude to God, as well
as his concern for the welfare of the people,
would doubtlefs prompt him to communi-

ᵘ Vide MANETH. apud. JOSEPH. contra APION. lib. I. § 14.
And BRYANT's Obfervations, &c. p. 150.

I

cate

cate to them fo much of the true, genuine
religion, as they were capable of receiving,
and applying to their profit. If " he informed their princes after his will," he certainly could not forget to " teach their fe-
nators this true wifdom [x]." And whatever
ordinances he might think proper to make
in relation to this fubject; his reduction of
the feveral provinces into one kingdom
under the government of one monarch,
made it eafy for him to convey and eftablifh
them throughout the land. And that he
thought proper, in fact, to make fome decrees, and enact certain ftatutes, which, we
may juftly fuppofe, had reference to *religious*,
as well as *civil* matters, is exprefly afferted
of him [y]. Nor did his decrees fail of their
effect. For it is vifible, I think, on the face
of the hiftory, that the Egyptians became,
under his wife adminiftration, much better
men, and much better fubjects, than they
feem to have been before.

[x] Pfal. cv. 22.

[y] The Targums make frequent mention of the *decrees* or
ftatutes of Joseph.

If

If they fell off and degenerated afterwards; if, upon the acceſſion of a " new," and more arbitrary, " king into the throne of Egypt;" one " who *knew* not," that is, as Onkelos [z] explains it, " who *approved* not the ſtatutes of, Joſeph ;" if at this time, I ſay, they began to relapſe into vice and ſuperſtition ; how kindly and beneficently was it ordained by heaven, that the Iſraelites ſhould then dwell among them—hold up to them the light of truth—and ſhew them the paths of virtue and goodneſs ?

That the Iſraelites then kept firm to their religion, and held forth to their neighbours a good example (however they might afterwards be infeſted by them) is a point which admits of no diſpute.   It is plainly implied in the counſel of this " new king [a]," that, finding them a diſtinſt people, he had made ſome attempts to aboliſh the diſtinſtion ; to incorporate them with the reſt of the nation, and melt them down into the common maſs. But, in the ſure confidence they had, of being

[z] Targ. in Exod. i. 8.
[a] See Ex. i. 10. and the Commentators thereon.

brought

brought at length out of that land; their diftinction and religion they *would* still preserve.
And *this*, I apprehend, was the first and
chief occasion of their afflictions; though
afterwards aggravated on other accounts.
These afflictions however, among other ends,
afforded them fair and frequent opportunities of displaying many noble, though passive
virtues. And their dispersion through the
land [b] opened at the same time a still larger
and wider field, wherein they might sow the
seeds of religion. Nor did the seeds they
sowed entirely perish. They struck root
among the people; and produced at length
no inconsiderable harvest to the Lord. For
when the Israelites departed out of Egypt,
we are expresly told, that " a great multitude went also with them [c];" who are all,
with good reason, supposed, to have been so
many proselytes to the true religion.

[b] Exod. I. 11. 14.--V. 12.

[c] Exod. xii. 38. Heb. " A numerous mixture." The Targum
of JONATHAN makes them numerous indeed. Vide in loc. Of
these how many soever they were, STRABO, on the strength of
ancient tradition, says, that, " being instructed by Moses, they
renounced their idolatrous worship, and accompanied him in his
march out of Egypt." Geogr. lib. xvi p. 760, &c.

Thus

Thus then we fee, which was the point to be cleared, that the patriarchal difpenfation was gracioufly planned for the general benefit of the nations: that it was calculated to correct their idolatrous opinions, and to reform their vitiated manners : that it was defigned to infpire the heathens with a due fenfe of the being and providence of God ; and to confirm his peculiar and chofen people in the belief of the promifed Redeemer. In fhort, that it was meant and fitted for the improvement of all—to prepare the world for the reception of that grand bleffing, which was to be poured upon it in the fulnefs of time.

Ends thefe, great and good—truly worthy of their divine author ! and ends, which, accomplifhed, claim our warmeft and moft grateful praife.

Therefore, to God the Father, God the Son, and God the Holy Ghoft, be afcribed, as is moft due, all honour, glory, &c. *Amen.*

S E R-

S E R M O N IX.

JUDE, ver. 7.

Even as Sodom and Gomorrha, and the cities about them, in like manner giving themselves over to fornication, and going after strange flesh, are set forth for an example, suffering the vengeance of eternal fire.

IT was observed in a preceding Discourse, that the confusion of languages, and the division of nations consequent thereupon, were attended, among other effects, with this great and peculiar advantage—" that God could at any time, when a people became incurably wicked, cut them off by a signal destruction, deftruction, without hurting the reft of the world: nay, that their excifion might eventually ferve, as a kind warning to thofe around them, not to offend by the like crimes, for fear they fhould fall under the like punifhment[d]."

Now this we fee moft aftonifhingly verified in the cafe of the people mentioned in the text. For " Sodom and Gomorrha, and the cities about them, giving themfelves over to fornication, and going after ftrange flefh, are fet forth" to this day " for an example" to others; being entirely overthrown, and " fuffering the vengeance of eternal fire."

But before we come to explain the nature of this *cataftrophe*—to vindicate the goodnefs and juftice of God in fo dreadful an infliction—and to confider the propriety of it, with refpect to the ends it was intended to promote:—Before we come, I fay, to difcufs thefe points, we muft previoufly inveftigate the real character of the inhabitants of thefe cities, in order to difcover what kind

[d] Sermon VII. p. 18o.

of

of treatment their deeds and practices could equitably deferve.

Now, as it is well known, that this people was a branch of the defcendants of Ham; fo it may well be fuppofed, that they inherited fomething of the corrupt difpofition of the original ftock: upon which when they had ingrafted the principles of idolatry, it is eafy to perceive what a luxuriant crop of evil fruits would naturally fpring forth among them. For idolatry was ever the parent of vice: and it doubtlefs happened to *this*, as to all *other* people, that, " when they did not like to retain God in their knowledge, God gave them over to a reprobate mind; not only to do thofe things which are not convenient [e], but alfo to work all uncleannefs with greedinefs [f]."

By what fteps they proceeded to this excefs of wickednefs, and by what fpecial methods Providence attempted to correct their vices, we are not particularly informed: nor is it indeed to be expected we fhould, in fo

[e] Rom. i. 28.
[f] Eph. iv. 19.

concife a hiftory as that of Mofes. But that they did, however, actually proceed to fuch enormities, even in fpite of many and powerful motives to the contrary, this hiftory, concife as it is, has given us fufficient affurance.

When Lot came firft among them, it is exprefly faid, that " the men of Sodom were then wicked, and finners before the Lord, exceedingly [g] :" that they were men, who had rebelled againft the true God ; had fet up the worfhip of falfe deities [h]; and, in confequence of that worfhip, had plunged themfelves into all kinds of vice and immorality ;—even the deteftable practice of unnatural lufts.

But befides the influence of a falfe religion, there was another caufe which contributed greatly to the fame effect: and that was the fertility of their country. The abundance it produced, and the comforts it fupplied, rendered them proud and haughty—

[g] Gen. xiii. 13.

[h] Colebant cultum alienum, et rebellabant in nomen Domini. valde. Targ. in loc.

luxurious

luxurious and effeminate—and confequently prone to all thofe vices, which are apt to flow from fuch difpofitions. Hence the pro- phet Ezekiel, reproving Jerufalem for her wickednefs and idolatries, fays, "Behold, this was the iniquity of thy fifter Sodom— Pride, fulnefs of bread, and abundance of idle- nefs was in her, and in her daughters; neither did fhe ftrengthen the hand of the poor and needy. And they were haughty, and com- mitted *abomination* before me: therefore I took them away as I faw fit[i]." And fitting indeed it was, that the Lord fhould punifh them with peculiar feverity, when they obftinately continued their wicked practices in plain con- tradiction to thofe providential documents, that were kindly meant, and excellently adapted, to awaken their attention, and lead them to repentance and amendment of life. For that many fuch providences were ex- ercifed towards them, is apparent from the account, which the Scripture has given us of them.

[i] Ch. xvi. 49, 50.   See alfo JOSEPH. Ant. Jud. lib. I. c. xi. § 1.

P 2   When

When they began to pride themselves in their riches, and presumptuously to strengthen themselves in their wickedness; God brought upon them the king of Elam; who laid them under tribute, and held them in slavery *twelve* years [k]. This event, as it necessarily contributed to diminish their wealth; so it naturally tended to abate their pride, to suppress their luxury, to check their vices, and to quicken their powers in the various exercise of laudable industry. How far it operated to these good purposes, we cannot be certain: very probably in no high degree. For they were afterwards delivered into the hands of their enemies, who punished them, as well for their wickedness as their rebellion, by a grievous slaughter in the vale of Siddim—where numbers of them were killed; and the rest were carried away captive [l].

But in the midst of this severity, God still remembered mercy. For the captives were soon miraculously rescued, and brought back with all their goods, by that declared

[k] Gen. xiv. 4.
[l] Ibid. 8—11.

favourite

favourite of heaven, the holy patriarch Abraham.

Now this deliverance, which both Abraham and Melchizedek openly aſcribed, in their preſence, to " the moſt high God, the poſſeſſor of heaven and earth [m]," ought in reaſon to have worked on their gratitude—to have led them to eſteem this great God, as their guardian and protector—and to have engaged them for the future in his worſhip and ſervice.

To guide and encourage them in this ſervice they were providentially favoured with the example and converſation of Lot: A man, who was endowed with eminent virtues and great piety; a man, who had ſhewed himſelf their faithful friend and ſtedfaſt ally; a man, who was a near relation of that extraordinary perſon to whoſe kindneſs they were indebted for the recovery of their liberties, and the enjoyment of all they poſſeſſed; and conſequently a man, whoſe admonitions and remonſtrances would have had, one ſhould think, their proper

[m] Gen. xiv. 19, 20.

P 3

weight

weight and influence upon them. But the
return of power, and the influx of profperity
had fo far debauched their minds, and corrupted their hearts, that they were now become quite impatient of all reftraints, and
refolutely bent on the full gratification of
their vicious paffions. On therefore they
went without controul, to the forrow and
vexation of pious Lot, in their abominable
and pernicious courfes. " For that righteous
man," though he laboured to reclaim them
for *twenty* years, was unable at laft to make
any ferious impreffions upon them: but,
" feeing and hearing from day to day," the
repeated inftances of their profligate and
abandoned wickednefs, fruitlefly " tor-
mented his upright foul with their unlawful" and fcandalous " proceedings [n]—"
which rofe at length to fuch enormities,
as were truly grievous and intolerable. For
to fuch a degree of impudence and profligacy
were their actions now grown, that every
one, endowed with any fenfe of virtue, who
reads their hiftory with the leaft attention,

[n] 2 Pet. ii. 7, 8.

muft

must feel in his breast a strong and pungent indignation against them; and presage in his mind, that God, in vindication of his neglected justice, was bound to inflict some speedy and remarkable judgment upon them. Their guilt was heinous, habitual, and general. They were not only " abominable in their doings," but unanimously abominable too. They all combined together in the same detestable purpose. " The men of Sodom," says the text, " compassed the house around, both old and young, all the people from *every* quarter°." A combination, which proves them to be universally depraved, beyond imagination, and beyond recovery. For when all ranks of men unite in vice; when they commit those things openly, which " it is a shame even to speak of in secret;" when the youth have lost all reverence for the aged, and dare expose their guilt to them, whom, of all others, they should hide it from; when the aged have lost all reverence for themselves, and fear not to publish their shame to their sons, but

* Gen. xix. 4.

are rather forward to make them witnesses of their guilt and infamy: when this, I say, is the case; then is coruption evidently advanced to its laft ftage—that people is utterly abandoned—and, having no good principle left, that can be worked upon, is abfolutely ripe for deftruction [p].

And yet, even in this cafe, the Lord did not deftroy them abruptly; but firft communicated his intention to Abraham; and then allowed him to plead their caufe, and urge what he could in arreft of judgment. And furely their defence could never have been placed in better hands. For, with what delicacy of addrefs, with what foftnefs of extenuation, with what earneftnefs of folicitude, and with what conftancy of interceffion did he argue for them? His conduct is inimitable: And his concern and compaffion for this devoted people can only be equalled by the gracious condefcenfion of God; who mercifully admitted every plea, which Abraham thought proper to urge in their behalf. But Abraham had a proper fenfe, as well of

[p] Rev. exam. vol. II. diff. v. p. 222.

justice,

juftice, as of mercy; and wifely confidered, what was due to the majefty of God, as well as defirable on the part of man. And therefore when he perceived, that they were totally depraved; when their fpreading guilt had not left even the fmall number of " *ten* righteous men among them;" he patiently refigned them to the punifhment they de-ferved—concluding either from former ex-periences, or affured perhaps by particular promife, that favour would be fhewn to thofe few who had preferved their integrity; and that a way would be opened for their fafe deliverance. And here let it be obferved, that if the faithful, benevolent, and compaf-fionate Abraham found himfelf in equity obliged to give up the caufe of this aban-doned people; it muft certainly be fome other principle, than the fenfe of humanity, or the love of virtue, that can prompt men now to refume their defence; and arraign the juftice of God in their punifhment. But their efforts only prove, how miferably vice perverts the underftanding.

Now

Now, the crying guilt of thefe cities being fully proved, and expofed to the world, in this conference with Abraham; and there being nothing left, which the merciful patriarch could alledge farther in bar of judgment; " the Lord" then opened the ftorehoufe of vengeance; and " rained down upon Sodom and Gomorrah fire and brimftone out of heaven: and thereby overthrew thofe cities, and all the plain, and all the inhabitants of the cities, and every thing that grew upon the ground. And lo, the fmoke of the country went up as the fmoke of a furnace q."

This tremendous event, thus notified before-hand, and attended with fuch marvellous circumftances, carried in it a plain indication of its being brought about, not merely by the fettled agency of fecond caufes, (though fome of thefe will appear to have been very properly made ufe of in it) but by the direct and immediate exertion of a divine power: and for the timely punifhment of that abandoned race.

q Gen. xix. 24, 25. 28.

Should

Should it here be demanded, " why God fhould choofe to punifh them in this, rather than in any other manner—" We return for anfwer, that, though there might be fome reafons for it, which we cannot difcover; yet are there others, obvious enough, which fufficiently juftify the wifdom of Providence; and fet forth the propriety of this mode of punifhment in a very confpicuous light.

If they worfhiped the *heavens*, and paid adoration to *lights* and *meteors*; how fully muft they, and the nations around them, be taught and convinced by this act, that God ruleth in the heavens above, as well as on the earth beneath; and that he can, when he pleafes, make " wind and ftorm, thunder and lightning," the minifters of his vengeance on a finful people?

If the fertility of their country, and the plenty it produced, contributed to excite and inflame their paffions; and alfo to fupport them in their profligate indulgences; how wifely was it ordained—as a lafting memorial of God's difpleafure againft all rioting,

luxury,

luxury, and intemperance—that the whole region should be burnt up, and rendered for the future utterly steril? And how aptly were the nations thence instructed, that it was the firm and settled purpose of Providence, whenever his bounties came to be abused, to " make a fruitful land defolate and barren, for the wickednefs of them that dwell therein [r]?"

And fince the people were all devoted to deftruction; in how fpeedy a manner, and with what frugal difplay of extraordinary power, was it brought upon them, by adjufting the means, as here defcribed, to the nature and conftitution of the foil? For that region, abounding with *bitumen*, was no fooner ftruck by the lightning, than it kindled into a flame; and fuffocated the inhabitants by its noxious exhalations. Then the fire, running along the veins of this inflammable matter into the caverns below, rarified the air, and produced a violent earthquake; whereby the cities were inftantly overturned: and the ground, at the fame

[r] Pf. vii. 34.

time,

time, finking down, formed a deep and extenfive cavity; which, being foon filled by
the influx of waters, became a fea; " and
covered all the plain." So quickly and
compendioufly was the defolation completed—which fufficiently accounts for this
mode of proceeding.

But the propriety of it will ftill farther
appear from the ufes that were intended to
be ferved by it.

And it was one intention of this fignal
cataftrophe, to imprefs upon the nations
(what they much wanted to have impreffed
upon them) a full conviction of God's immediate and conftant infpection into the affairs
and concerns of mankind,[*]—a full conviction
of his not contenting himfelf with governing
the world by what we call a general providence, and the eftablifhed order of things;
but of his actually interpofing in a moft exact
and particular manner to punifh fome particular, enormous fins: to imprefs upon them
a full conviction, that, however patient and

[*] Vide Targ. in Gen. xix. 24. Non fecerunt pœnitentiam,
quoniam dixerunt, non manifefta funt coram Domino opera mala.

forbearing

forbearing he might be for a time; yet, when the iniquities of men were come to the full, he would finally appear as terrible in his judgments, as they were vile and abominable in their doings. And that such a conviction was accordingly made and impressed upon them, is evident from the case of Abimelech; who, having ignorantly taken another man's wife, and being consequently in danger of committing a crime, which bore some affinity to the sins of Sodom, was afterwards mightily concerned for his land, lest God should destroy it in a similar manner [t].

Hence then we are led to the consideration of another end, that was proposed to be answered by this *cataftrophe*. It served as a caution to the several nations, not to indulge the same crimes, for fear they should fall under the same punishment. And it is accordingly held up continually to their view, in the sacred writings, by way of check and terrour. Thus the prophets, in their addresses to Babylon, Jerusalem, and other

[t] Gen. xx. 7, 8, 9.

profane

profane and impious cities, often remind
them of this event; and as often threaten
them, that, if they did not forſake the errour of their ways, they ſhould be ſo pu-
niſhed and fearfully overthrown, " as when
God overthrew Sodom and Gomorrah ."
Thus alſo the Pſalmiſt, diſſuading the ungodly from their perverſe doings, plainly
refers them to this miraculous infliction,
both as a proof and example of that divine
vengeance, which awaits notorious and im-
penitent ſinners. However ſecure they may
think themſelves, yet juſtice will certainly
overtake them; and " they ſhall finally receive the due reward of their deeds." For
" upon the wicked," ſays he, " God will
rain ſnares," or quick burning coals, " fire
and brimſtone, ſtorm and tempeſt. This
ſhall be their portion to drink ."

Now as this event was ſo admirably calculated to check the career of unthinking
ſinners, and engage their attention to their

Deut. xxix. 22--24. Iſ. xiii. 19. Jer. xxiij. 14—xlix. 18.—
l. 40. Ez. xxxviii. 22. Amos iv. 11. Zeph. ii. 9.
x Pſ. xi. 6.

moſt

moft important concerns; how wifely was it provided, that the memory of it fhould be conveyed to pofterity, not only by the lefs affecting reprefentation of hiftory, but alfo by the more amazing vifible corufcations of perpetually living fire? For that this region continued to burn for ages, we find attefted by feveral authors of great and undoubted credit.

To pafs by the author of the book of Wifdom [y], Diodorus Siculus, who lived in the reign of Julius Cæfar, defcribing the Afphaltite lake, which now occupies all that fpace where thefe ruined cities formerly ftood, tells us, " that the country about it was *then* on fire; and fent forth a grievous fmell; to which he attributes the fickly conftitution and fhort lives of the neighbouring inhabitants [z]."

Strabo, who flourifhed foon after, mentions likewife the fea of Sodom by the miftaken name of *lacus Serbonis*; and " fpeaks of it as bubbling and emitting *fmoke* at the

[y] See ch. x. 6--9.
[z] Bib. Hift. lib. xix.

5

time

time he wrote——"; and moreover adds, that " the broken and burnt rocks, ruins of buildings, and cineritious earth, which are feen all about it, give credit to the teftimony of the people of the country, who fay, that Sodom and the other cities, which anciently ftood in this place, were deftroyed by earth-quake and fire [a]."

Tacitus gives nearly the fame account; and afferts, that " the traces of the fire were ftill vifible in the burnt earth [b]."

From thefe teftimonies it evidently appears, and ftill more particularly from the teftimony of Philo [c], that this fire lafted, without intermiffion, till after the days of the Apoftles. And if fo, we may eafily account for the phrafeology of the text; where St. Jude obferves of Sodom and Gomorrah, that " they are fet forth as an example, fuffering the vengeance of ETERNAL fire [d]."

[a] Geograph. lib. x.
[b] Hiftor. lib. v.
[c] Vit. Mof. lib. ii. fub finem.
[d] Ver. 7.

For a fire, which was actually burning at the time he wrote; and had continued to burn for near two thousand years together [e], sufficiently justifies the Apostle's language in applying to it *that* epithet.—It justifies also the application and sentiment of another Apostle, in making it the emblem of that *everlasting* punishment, which is reserved for the wicked in another life. For thus St. John, in plain allusion to the subject before us, describes the future state of the ungodly, and the misery they are to suffer in the other world—" Their part shall be in the *lake*, which burneth with fire and brimstone [f].—And the *smoke* of their torment ascendeth up for ever and ever [g]."

Nor was this emblematical use of it, as a representation of God's eternal ven-

[e] Yea and is probably burning *now*. For BROCHART, who visited this lake in the twelfth century, saw it then " flaming and smoking like the mouth of hell." Descrip. Ter. Sanctæ, p. 1. cap. viii. § 35. And later travellers have observed something of the like appearance, in proportion to the quantity of the floating bitumen.

[f] Rev. xxi. 8.

[g] Ibid. xiv. 11.

geance,

geance, on the impieties of mankind, confined to the limits of divine revelation. It was fo apt, pertinent, and ftriking, that it gained admittance into the heathen mythology. For the poetic rivers of hell, the *black Cocytus,* and the *burning Phlegethon,* feem to be only, if I may fo fpeak, ftreams derived from the *Dead fea.* But neverthelefs, fince thefe fabled rivers, as well as the fea to which they refer, ferved to work on the apprehenfions of men, and thereby to reftrain them from vicious practices; they fo far anfwered the intention of Providence, and confpired with his other difpenfations to the general improvement and happinefs of the world.

The practical conclufions, which refult from the whole, and which juftly merit our regard, are thefe.

That " the Lord alloweth or approveth the righteous; but the ungodly, and him that delighteth in wickednefs, doth his foul abhor [h]."

h Pfal. xi. 6. old verfion.

Q 2

That

That though " he is merciful and long-
fuffering, not willing that any fhould perifh,
but that all fhould come to repentance[1];"
yet, if men will perverfly continue in fin,
and abufe the means of falvation; " his
wrath" will certainly burft out, and fall
heavily at laft " on thofe children of vice
and difobedience[k]." And therefore,

That it is no lefs our intereft, than it
is our duty, to confider thefe things in
time; and make all the hafte we poffibly can, to fecure, by a courfe of virtue, both our prefent peace, and our future
felicity.

And when once we are engaged in
this courfe, let us " remember Lot's wife[l];"
and take heed, that we neither " turn
again," nor " look back" to the things we
have left behind us. For fhe ftands, not
only as a woful inftance of the wondrous manner, in which the wicked inha-

[1] 2 Pet. iii. 9.
[k] Ephef. v. 6.
[l] Luke xvii. 32. Gen. xix. 26.

bitants

bitants of that country perifhed; but alfo
as a lafting example to others, of the great
folly of delay and remiffnefs in their obedience to the commands of God.

Now to God the Father, &c.

SERMON X.

PSALM lxxviii. 12.

Marvellous things did he in the fight of their fathers in the land of Egypt, in the field of Zoan.

WE have feen the Ifraelites marvel-loufly conducted into the land of Egypt, and providentially fettled in the diftrict of Gofhen; where, though they lived diftinct by themfelves, they had yet many and frequent opportunities of imparting fomething of the true religion to all the people around them.

Q 4

Here

Here they continued above two hundred years; during which time, great and momentous revolutions happened, as well in the general ftate of the kingdom, as in their own particular affairs.

In the firft period of their fettlement; whilft-they comfortably enjoyed the benign influence of royal favour; as they were gratefully difpofed to inftruct thofe, with whom they converfed, in the true knowledge of God and his providence; fo their correfpondents, we may prefume, were no lefs inclined to be taught and inftructed by them. From thefe mutually good difpofitions, from thefe kind intercourfes and friendly correfpondence, great improvements muft necef-farily arife. For religion and virtue, ftrongly inculcated on one fide, and readily embraced on the other, muft naturally thrive and increafe: And, as they fpread, muft naturally and of courfe gather ftrength.

But whatever improvements the Egyptians might make in their religious fentiments or moral conduct, during this calm and aufpicious period; yet, certain it is, that

in

in fubfequent, and probably turbulent, times, when a new and impious king had acquired the dominion over them, they gradually re-lapfed into their former ftate of vice and ig-norance; and became again unhappily dif-tinguifhed by their grofs fuperftitions and abominable idolatries. For it is inconteftably evident, that in the days of Mofes they were entirely devoted to the worfhip and fervice of falfe deities: And not only fo, but that the Ifraelites themfelves, who fojourned among them, were in like manner, notwith-ftanding the promifes and feal of circum-cifion, either led by their example, or forced by their cruelty, to adopt and practife the fame fuperftitions [m].

When things were come to fuch a pafs; when this people, who had been raifed up on purpofe to preferve religion, were thus in danger of being perverted from it, or of perifhing under the afflictions which they fuffered on its account; when this, I fay, appears to be the cafe; was it not highly

[m] Exod. xxxii. 1—9. Jofh. xxiv. 14. Ezek. xx. 7, 8.—xxiii. 3. See Bp. WARBURTON'S Div. Leg. b. iv. § 6.

neceffary

neceffary that God fhould vifibly interpofe in their favour, and deliver them from the hands of their cruel, oppreffive, and infectious mafters? And confidering the part, which the Ifraelites had to act, in carrying on the defigns of his providence ; was it not equally neceffary, that the mode of their deliverance fhould be fo contrived, as to convince them and the reft of the world, that the notions they had imbibed were vain and erroneous, and the gods they adored falfe and ima-ginary?

Now, as thefe things were not only worthy of the divine cognizance in them-felves, but feem, in their very nature, to require fome proper provifion to be made for them; fo it is obfervable, that God, through the courfe of his manifeftations in Egypt, had a clear and conftant regard to them[n]. For the chief intention, as the Scripture af-

---

[n] Cum id ageret Deus, ut populum ab Ægypti fervitute li-beraret; ita parata funt omnia, ut Deus Ifraelis Ægypti deos ludibrio exponeret, cofque, una cum cultu eorum, vanitatis poft natos homines maxime redargueret. SPENCER de Leg. Heb, lib. I. c. i. § 1.

fures

fures us, of his " multiplying thofe figns
and wonders, both in heaven above, and in
the earth beneath," was to convince all—
the Ifraelites[o], Egyptians[p], and the reft of
the nations[q]—that " the heavens and the
earth were the Lord's, and that he was the
governor among all people[r];" or, in other
words, that " he alone was the true God,
and that there was none elfe befides him."—
How properly thefe manifeftations were
adapted to produce fuch convictions, I fhall
now endeavour to explain.

It is the fundamental principle of divine
government, to work upon rational creatures
in a rational manner. But the moft rational
method of reclaiming any people from the
errours they have imbibed, and of bringing
them over to the oppofite truths, is, to
make it plain to their underftanding, that
things are in fact juft the reverfe of what
they conceive; and to render them fenfible,

[o] Exod. vi. 7.—x. 2.
[p] Exod. vii. 5.—xiv. 4. 18.
[q] Exod. ix. 16.
[r] Pfal. xxij. 28.

that

that it were therefore more becoming their nature, as well as more conducive to their happiness, to think and act differently for the future.

Now, let us apply this to the cafe before us.

Mankind were never fo depraved in their notions of the divinity, but they attributed to it as well the government and conduct of things, as the diftribution of the good or ill that befel them: And fo far they were certainly right. But then they falfly imagined, that the more illuftrious and active parts of the univerfe—the fun, ftars, and elements— completely anfwered thefe divine characters. For, as they obferved the courfe of things to be conftantly regulated, and the bleffings and calamities of life to be daily difpenfed, by the motion and agency of thefe bodies; fo they were led, by thofe appearances, to believe them to be the only gods that governed the world. Herein lay their ruinous miftake. And by what means was this miftake to be corrected? Was it not by convincing them, that thefe bodies had no other

powers

powers or qualities, than what they derived from their great Creator; whofe inftruments they were in carrying on the purpofes of his providence? And what properer method could Jehovah employ to form in their minds this conviction, than that of empowering his minifter to change or fupprefs the qualities of fuch bodies; and make them operate, by his bare command, in direct oppofition to their ordinary courfe?

This was to appeal to their own notions; to make them fenfible in their own way, that he alone was the governour of the world; and that all vifible beings were but fo many fubordinate agents, working by his power, and under his direction; and confe-quently, that he alone was intitled to the worfhip and obedience of men, as he alone could reward or punifh them.

Now, as fuch a procefs was moft aptly accommodated, in the reafon of things, to the circumftances and apprehenfions of man-kind; fo, in the cafe of the Egyptians, the Deity, we find, proceeded accordingly—exerting his power in appropriated inftances, which equally ferved to demonftrate the nullity of the gods they worfhiped, as to punifh the crimes they had been guilty of in confequence of that worfhip.

But, to fet this matter in a clear light, it will be neceffary to take a particular view of the progrefs and conduct of the whole procedure.

In the firft place then, Jehovah, by a meffage in his own name, required the Egyptians to releafe his people[s]. The Egyptians difclaimed all knowledge of him, and arrogantly difdained to pay any regard or attention to him. " Who is Jehovah," replied Pharaoh, " that I fhould obey his voice, to let Ifrael go? I know not Jehovah, neither will I let Ifrael go[t]." They had gods of their own—*univerfal nature* and its feveral *parts*[v]—who could, they thought, act as power-

[s] Exod. v. 1.

[t] Ibid. ver. 2.

[v] They worfhiped the *univerfe* under the name, 1. of Pan. Παρ' Αἰγυπτίοισι δὲ, ΠΑΝ μὲν, ἀρχαιότατο κỳ τῶν ὀκτὼ τῶν πρώτων λεγομένων Θεῶν εἶναι. HEROD. Euterp. c. cxlv. And of him it is fung, —— Πᾶνα

powerfully in their behalf, as Jehovah could do in behalf of the Ifraelites. In thefe therefore they trufted, aud upon thefe they depended.

This then, you fee, was the proper time to convince them of their folly; or to punifh their ftubbornnefs, if they proved incorrigible. But God, foreknowing what the confequence would be, and unwilling to enter on the methods of feverity, commanded his fervants to go again to Pharaoh, and repeat the demand of his difmiffing the Ifraelites. Upon this fecond application, the king required them to exhibit fome miracle, as a

---

Πᾶνα καλῶ κραΐερὸν—κόσμοιο. τὸ σύμπαν,
Οὐρανὸν, ἠδὲ θάλασσαι, ἰδὲ χθόνα παμβασίλειαι,
Καὶ πῦρ ἀθάναἴον· τάἴε γὰρ μέλη ἐςὶ τὰ Πανός.
ORPH. Hym. in Pan.

2. under that of Serapis; Nam Serapis, quem Ægyptii deum maximum prodide erunt, oratus a Nicocreonte Cypriorum rege quis deorum haberetur, his verfibus follicitam religionem regis inftruxit——

Εἰμὶ θεὸς τοιόσδε μαθεῖν, οἷον κ᾽ ἐγὼ εἴπω·
Οὐράνι©- κόσμ©- κεφαλὴ, γαςὴρ δὲ θάλασσα,
Γαῖα ἔ μοι πόδις εἰσὶ, τὰ δ᾽ ὄατ᾽ ἐν αἰθέρι κεῖται,
Ὀμμά τε τηλαυγὲς λαμπρὸν φά©- ἠελίοιο.
MACROB. Saturn. Lib. I. c. xx.

proof

proof that Jehovah was really God, and that they were charged with his commiſſion. Aaron, in compliance with that requeſt, " threw down his rod before Pharaoh, and before his ſervants, and it became a ſerpent ˣ—" which in their *hieroglyphical* theology, was the emblem or repreſentation of the *ſupreme* God ʸ." Hereupon the magicians were called to confront him ; who, being arrived, inſtantly " threw down every man his rod, which became in like manner ſerpents—" emblems or ſymbols of their ſupreme divinities. Thus far both parties might be thought, perhaps, to have exhibited equal ſigns of power. But the ſuperiority ſoon appears: for " Aaron's rod ſwallowed up all the rods of the magicians ᶻ." An evident prognoſtic this, of the event of the enſuing conteſt; wherein Jehovah vanquiſhed and

---

ˣ Exod. vii. 10.

ʸ Οἱ Ἀιγύπλιοι—τὸν δὲ ΟΦΙΝ, ἀγαθὸν Δαίμονα σημαίνοντες, i. e. Ægyptii Serpente bonum Dæmonem ſignificant. SANCHO-NIATH. apud EUSEB. Præp. Ev. Lib. I. c. x. p. 41. &c. Voss. de Idololatr. lib. III. cap. 15. in fine.

ᶻ Exod. viii. 12.

deſtroyed

deſtroyed all the gods of Egypt in reality, as he did here in ſymbols.

This miracle making no impreſſion on the minds of Pharaoh and his miniſters, God then proceeded to exert his power in ſtill more awakening miracles—ſuch as not only proved, that he was " God of gods, and Lord of lords," but alſo ſhewed, that " his power and his wrath is againſt all them that forſake him [a]."

Theſe miracles, though ſeemingly con-fuſed to ſuperficial readers, may nevertheleſs, upon cloſer inſpection, be eaſily reduced into *four claſſes*; as being tranſacted in the *four elements*, which were eſteemed in Egypt the four principal deities.

Let us then conſider them in their order: for there is plainly a regular order, and a juſt gradation, obſervable in them.

I. The Egyptians, it is well known, held WATER [b] in high veneration; and more par-

[a] Ezra viii. 22.

[b] Ægypti incolæ aquarum beneficia percipientes, aquam colunt, aquas ſuperſtitioſa votorum continuatione venerantur. JUL. FIRMIC. de Er. prof. Religionis. PHIL. Jud. de vita Moſis, lib. i. p. 617.

ticularly the river Nile[c]. This was the fruitful fource of their choiceft bleffings; and
thence became the chief object of their religious regard. For, as their daily fuftenance
was, in a great meafure, owing to its
bounty—its water being their common
drink, and its fifh their common food[d]; fo
were they punctually careful in paying it
their conftant and daily devotions. If then
they were to be convinced, that " God is
wonderful in the waters;" that *that* river in
particular was his[e]; and that they ought to
be thankful to him for it; furely his depriv-
ing it of all its utility—deftroying its fifh
that they might not eat them, altering its

[c] Οὐδὲν γὰρ ὕτω τιμὴ Αἰγυπίοις ὡς ὁ Νεῖλος.   Nihil enim apud
Ægyptios tanto in honore erat atque Nilus. PLUT. de If. et
Ofir. § 5.

[d] Numbers xi. 5. HERODOT. Eut. c. lxxvii. DIOD. SIC.
Bib. Hift. lib. I. p. 32. Ed. Hanov.

[e] The prefent king of Egypt might perhaps imagine, with the
fame arrogance as one of his fucceffors afterwards did—See Ezek.
xxix. 3.---that this river was fo peculiarly and emphatically his
own, that it was not in the power of any God to difpoffefs or de-
prive him of its benefits.

water

water that they could not drink it f—was
no unlikely means to work that effect.—
And if they were, which they are said to
have been, so barbarously superstitious in
their devotions to this river, as, at a particular period in every year, to stain its current
with human sacrifices g; then his " turning
its water into blood" was a just and suitable
punishment for such bloody cruelties h.

Then again, as the banks of this river
were the grand scene of their magical operations i, in which blood and *frogs* made the
principal part of the apparatus k; so, by
commanding it to produce such an infinite

---

f PHILO (vit. Mosis, lib. i. p. 617. Ed. Paris.) seems to inti-
mate, that the fish became immediately unfit for use; their nutri-
tive property being instantly changed into another of the most
pestiferous nature. And JOSEPHUS says (Antiq. Jud. lib. ii
c. xiv. § 1.) that the water brought great pains and bitter tor-
ments upon those who ventured to drink of it.

g Universal Hist. vol. I. b. I. ch. iii. § 1. p. 413 and
484. 8vo.

h Ex. vii. 19. 21. Rev. xvi. 5. 6.

i Targ. JON. B. UZIEL. in Exod. vii. 15. et viii. 16.

k MAIMON. Mor. Nevoch. p. iii. c. xlvi. SPENCER de Leg
Heb. lib. ii. c. xv. § 1. HORAT. Epod. v. ver. 19. JUVENAL.
Sat. iii. ver. 44.

multi-

multitude of thefe creatures to annoy them[1], he adapted his chaſtiſement to the nature of their crimes: adapted it indeed in a moſt wonderful manner: ſince frogs were not only the inſtruments of their abominations, but likewiſe the emblems of thoſe impure dæmons, whom they invoked by their incantations[m].

II. The EARTH was another object of their worſhip[n]; to which they addreſſed their ſolemn devotions, and offered up the firſt fruits of the harveſt, as to the donor of their corn and grain, and of all the other produce of the year[o]. To make them therefore ſen-

[1] Exod. viii. 5. 6.

[m] Rev. xvi. 13.

[n] Non eoſdem deos ſimiliter colunt univerſi Ægyptii, πλὴν Ἰσιός τι, κ) Ὀσίριος, præter Iſidem et Oſirin—hos peræque univerſi colunt. HERODOT. Euterp. c. 42. Ἰσιδος σῶμα Γῆν ἔχεσι κ) νομίζεσιν. PLUT. de Iſ. et Oſ. § 38.

[o] Ἔτι γὰρ κ) νῦν καλὰ τὸν θερισμὸν τὰς πρώτας ἀμηθέντας σάχυς, κ. τ. λ. Nam etiam nunc meſſis tempore oblatis ſpicarum primitiis, incolæ juxta manipulos plangere, Iſidemque invocare ſolent. Id quod idcirco faciunt, ut honorem pro inventis Deæ ſub primæ inventionis tempus retribuant. DIOD. SICUL. Bib. Hiſt. lib. i. p. 13. EUSEB. Præp. Evang. lib. iii. cap. vi. ſub fin. SPENCER de Leg. Heb. lib. iii. cap. xi.

ſible,

ſible, that the EARTH did not put forth thoſe life-ſuſtaining productions (for which they adored it with miſtaken gratitude) by any independent virtue of its own, but only in conſequence of the divine eſtabliſhment; to make them, I ſay, ſenſible of this, God reverſed the nature of its productions; cauſing it to "bring forth *lice* on man and beaſt, through all the land of Egypt[p]." Before, they were nouriſhed by what the earth produced; now, they are devoured by it.

"And becauſe they had gone aſtray ſo very far in the ways of errour, as to hold the cattle of the field—yea, noiſome beaſts, reptiles, and inſects—for gods[q];" therefore the former were killed by a murrain[r]; and a mixture of the latter was ſent to torment them[s]: "that they might experimentally know,

[p] Exod. viii. 16, 17.

[q] Wiſd. xi. 15.

[r] Exod. ix. 3—6.

[s] Exod. viii. 21—24. *Heb.* הערב, which the *Vulg.* renders, omne genus muſcarum; but the LXX more particularly, κυνόμυιαν,

know, that wherewithal a man finneth, by
the fame alfo fhall he be punifhed ᵗ."

III. The AIR was another of their chief
divinities ᵘ; to whom they attributed the fa-
lubrity of their climate, and the healthinefs
of their own conftitutions ˣ; and whofe benevolence therefore they ftudied to engage
by the offerings of daily incenfe ʸ. To convince them of the falfhood of this opinion;
to fhew them, that " God alone woundeth
and healeth, killeth and maketh alive;" he
changed the falubrious qualities of the air,
and rendered it peftilential—" exciting hot,
inflamed tumors, and virulent, angry ulcers,
both in man and beaft, throughout all the

---

i. e. *dog-fly*. And in this fenfe, the infliction is juftly applicable
to a particular branch of their fuperftition, viz. *dog-worfhip.*
Oppida tota canem venerantur. Juv. Sat. xv. ver. 8.

ᵗ Wifd. xi. 16.

ᵘ Τὸν δ' Ἀέρα προσαγορεῦσαι φασὶν Ἀθηνᾶν, κ. τ. λ. Aëri porro
Minervæ nomen, quadam vocis interpretatione, attribuiffe, Jo-
vifque filiam hanc et virginem putari, eo quod aer natura corrup-
tioni non fit obnoxius. DIODOR. SICUL. Bib. Hift. lib. i. p. 12.
EUSEB. Præp. Evang. lib. III. cap. ii.

ˣ HERODOT. Eut. c. lxxvii.

ʸ PLUTARCH. de Is. et Of. § 80.

land."

land."—And if you fuppofe this painful infliction to affect more particularly the ingui-
nal parts, as the word which we tranflate
" blains^z " feems to indicate ; we may then
conclude it to be farther intended as a juft
punifhment of thofe lafcivious practices, and
abominable impurities, to which the nation
was horribly addicted^a.

Then again; as they afcribed the exube-
rance, growth, and maturity of all vegetable
productions to the genial warmth and benign
influence of this divinity, the AIR ; fo the
Lord ftrengthned and invigorated the powers
of that element^b to correct and reprove their
errour.   For he caufed it to produce fuch

---

^z Exod. ix. 9. Heb. אבעבועת ulcera, apoftemata, morbus
gallicus.   Schindler in Rad. בעה.   Sic. et *Arab.* in fignif. 7.
Scortata fuit *mulier.*

^a Haud dubie *fornicandi* verbum, ut paffim, ad idololatriam
refertur. Ita tamen, ut fimul alludat ad *Ægyptiorum* libidines
impuriffimas. Horrefco referens. In parte hircini cultus id fuit,
quod quædam mulieres, tanquam religioni addictæ, facris fcilicet
hircis fœde fe fubmittebant. Bochart. Hieroz. p. I. lib. ii.
c. liii. See Levit. xviii. 23, 24.———xx. 15, 16. and Patrick's
Com. on the Texts.

^b Wifd. xvi. 24.

R 4   dreadful

dreadful ftorms of rain, hail, thunder, and lightning, as had never been known fince the foundation of Egypt; whereby the greateft part of the herbage and fruit was blafted and deftroyed.—And afterwards, the *eaft-wind,* which they likewife adored, conveyed through their coafts a large flight of locufts, to eat and confume the remainder [c].

IV. The fupreme objects of their worfhip were the SUN, MOON, and STARS [d], whofe fplendor ftruck them with high admiration, and whofe beneficence worked mightily upon their gratitude. To fhew them therefore that he ruled in the heavens, and governed thefe exalted and fplendid luminaries; Jehovah fufpended their lights and emanations—caufed them to withdraw their

[c] Exod. x. 12—15.

[d] Τὰς δ' ἐν κατ' Αἰγυπτίον ἀνθρώπας τὸ παλαιὸν γενομένας—ὑπολαβεῖν ἦναι δύο Θεὰς, αἰδίας τε κỳ πρώτας, τότε Ἥλιον κỳ τὴν Σελήνην, κ. τ. λ. Cæterum vetuftiffimos in Ægypto mortales—duos effe Deos exiftimaffe, æternos & primos, Solem quippe & Lunam; quorum illum Ofirim, hanc Ifim, appellarint. DIODOR. SICUL. Bibl. Hift. lib. I. p. 10. PORPHYR. apud EUSEB. Præp. Evang. lib. iii. cap. iv.

luftre

luftre—and " covered all the land of Egypt with thick darknefs for three days ᵉ."

To thefe miracles in proof of his fove-reignty, God fuperadded one more, as a de-monftration of his providence. For the death of every firft-born of the Egyptians carried fo lively a refemblance, and bore, as the author of the Book of Wifdom juftly obferves ᶠ, fo natural a relation to their fin, in deftroying every male of the Ifraelites; that they muft needs perceive, it was pur-pofely inflicted as a fuitable punifhment for that very cruelty: and confequently muft conclude, that this great and tremendous God, the God of Ifrael, took particular cog-nizance of human tranfactions; and, fooner or later, " rewarded every man according to his work."

Such were the miracles performed in Egypt; and fuch the purpofes intended by them. And, when viewed in this light; the very light in which the Scripture places

ᵉ Exod. x. 21---23.
ᶠ Ch. xviii. 5.

them;

3

them ; how judiciously do they appear to be
accommodated in their *nature* to the apprehenfions of the people, and the points in
controverfy ! how properly adapted, in every
refpect, to anfwer the ends, that were defigned by them ! Nor is the *manner* in which
they were wrought lefs worthy of our admiration ; fince it was fo calculated, as to ex-
clude or obviate every objection, which their
prejudices might fuggeft; and to forward
and improve every good and pious emo-
tion, which their reflections might infpire.
For,

In the firft place, as the Egyptians, who
had very high notions of the art of forcery,
might probably imagine, that Mofes performed thefe miracles and prodigies by fome
fafcination[g]; fo their own magicians were
freely permitted to try the utmoft of their
fkill and power in the repetition or imitation
of them: but they tried in vain. Their
acknowledged inability therefore to equal

[g] Origen contra Celsum, lib. iii. Philo Jud. De vita
Mofis lib. i.

and

and imitate them, plainly proved and inconteftably evinced, that they were not the
effects of magic, but the works of God [h].
And, though thefe deteftable feducers had fo
far impofed upon the people, as to make
them believe, that they could, by their incantations, fecure both their perfons and
properties from all kinds of evil [i]; yet, how
muft even the fimpleft among them, be now
awakened into a full conviction of the falfhood and vanity of fuch deceits, when they
faw the magicians, with all their boafting,
equally involved in the common calamities;
and, in fpite of the high pretenfions of their
art, fharing the general fate of their neighbours [k]! And this, it fhould feem, the hiftorian has been careful to record, left the
children of Ifrael fhould be led aftray, and
impofed upon by the like pretenfions.

Moreover, the Egyptians were forewarned
of the day, when every plague fhould befal

[h] Exod. viii. 19.
[i] MAIMON. Mor. Nevoch. p. iii, c. xxxvii.
[k] Wifd. xvii. 7. 8.

them;

them; and permitted to affign their own time, when they would have them removed: whereby they might clearly fee, that God alone was the author both of their fufferings and deliverances; and that no planetary afpect (for they thought the ftars governed the world) was fo favourable or malign, but that he could afflict or relieve them, when ever he pleafed.

Befides, thefe miraculous judgments came upon them by leifurely advances; and proper intervals of refpite were allowed them, to confider and reflect upon what had been done;—" that, feeing by their punifhment wherein they had offended, they might return from their wickednefs, and believe on the Lord [1]."

And laftly, to convince them that the God, who wrought thefe wonders among them, was the God of Ifrael; he made an obvious, vifible diftinction, through the courfe of his procedure, between the two nations: and whilft the land of Egypt was

[1] Wifd. xii, 2.

afflicted

afflicted with thefe plagues, the land of Gofhen, where the Ifraelites dwelt, remained free and unmolefted [m]. From whence they might draw this farther conclufion, that he was as truly gracious to the faithful and obedient, as he was terribly fevere on the rebellious and ungodly.

Now, if thefe rational methods of conviction could not prevail on the obftinate Egyptians to repent of their wickednefs, and let Ifrael go; what elfe can reafonably be expected, but that God, in juftice, fhould fuffer their crime to become their punifhment; and leave them " to eat the bitter fruit of their own ways, and to be filled with their own devices [n]?" Accordingly, when they purfued the Ifraelites, with infatuated refolution, into the midft of the fea; God, who was in no wife bound to preferve his enemies by a miracle, fuffered the fea to return to its ftrength—and overwhelm them all [o].

[m] Ex. viii. 22.—ix. 4. 26.—x. 23.—xii. 13.
[n] Prov. i. 31.
[o] Ex. xiv. 27, 28.

" Thus

" Thus the Lord got him honour upon Pharaoh, upon his chariots, and upon his horfemen—and likewife upon his gods[p];" whom, according to the cuftom of thofe ancient times, it is probable, he carried in the front of his army [q].

I need not obferve what awful impreffions this amazing judgment [r] muft fix on the minds of the feveral nations, to whom it became known; and how forcibly it muft convince them, that the God, who could do fuch mighty wonders, muft be " greater than all gods: fince, in the place and things, wherein they were fup-

---

[p] Ex. xiv. 18. Numb. xxxiii. 4.

[q] Familiare fuit idololatris antiquioribus, iter præfertim fufcepturis, aut cum hofte congreffuris, idola parvula fecum ferre; ut itineris focios, pugnæque duces atque aufpices haberent deos tutelares, iifque præfentibus cultum exhiberent. SPENCER. de Leg. Heb. Lib. iii. c. iii. § 1. Of this cuftom we meet with feveral inftances in Scripture; and with one even fo low as the days of David. 1 Chron. xiv. 12.

[r] And perhaps the more awful, becaufe of the *manner* in which it was accomplifhed. For the ancients accounted *drowning* a dreadful and accurfed death. Δεινὸν δ' ἰσὶ θανῶ μετὰ κύμασιν. HESIOD. Op. et Dier. lib. ii. ver. 305.

poſed to have moſt power, he was now found to be above them [s]."

But I muſt not, however, forget to mention, that this remarkable puniſhment, ſevere as it was on Pharaoh and his army, might yet be inflicted in great goodneſs, and be ultimately attended with great benefits, reſpecting the nation at large. For, if the various modes of idolatry, then practiſed in Egypt, were, as there is ſome reaſon to ſuſpect, impoſed upon the people by the *prieſts*, and ſupported by the *ſoldiery*; then, the total deſtruction of theſe oppreſſive agents of wickedneſs happily ſerved—to ſet the people at full liberty to judge for themſelves; and to follow the impulſe of thoſe reflections, which the preceding miracles had excited in their minds. But thoſe reflections would naturally lead them, to conſider Jehovah, the author of theſe miracles, as the only great and true God— and conſequently, as the ſole Being, to whom their veneration was to be now directed. Hence their religion muſt neceſ-

[s] Ex. xviii. 11.

farily

farily affume a new form ; and become, of courfe, more pure, perfect, and refined, than it was before. Being reformed themfelves, they communicated their improvements to other nations: for moft nations learnt of them—imbibed their fentiments, and copied their manners.

Now, if the cafe was really fuch; if the greateft part of the world derived their policy and religion from the Egyptians; then the reformation of the inhabitants of Egypt might eventually become the re-formation of the inhabitants of the greateft part of the globe.—A circumftance, which converts the feverity of this punifhment, into an inftance of benevolence of the moft extenfive kind.

" O the depth of the riches both of the wifdom and knowledge of God! how un-fearchable are his judgments, and his ways paft finding out!" *Amen.*

'Rom. xi. 33.

S E R-

SERMON XI.

DEUT. xxxii. 9, 10.

*The Lord's portion is his people, Jacob is the
lot of his inheritance.*

*He found him in a desert land, and in the
waste howling wilderness; he led him about,
he instructed him, he kept him as the apple of
his eye.*

THOUGH the children of Israel, in
consequence of the miracles they had
seen in Egypt, and of the wonderful passage
that was opened for them through the Red-
Sea, did now believe and gratefully ᵘ acknow-

ᵘ Exod. xiv. 31. Psal. cvi. 12.

VoL. I.   S   ledge,

ledge, that their great deliverer was the true God; and that he alone had a right to their obedience; yet, as their superstitious prejudices were deeply rooted, and their proneness to idolatry remained strong, the utmost precaution was still necessary to keep them from falling off. They were too weak and unsettled to be left to themselves, to contend with occurring temptations. For had they been allowed to converse familiarly with the neighbouring nations, or had they been conducted immediately into the land of Canaan, the very sight of the customary heathen worship would have rekindled their fondness for it; and its fascinating ceremonies would have seduced them again, to adopt and continue the practice of it.

To guard them therefore from the pernicious contagion of ill examples; and to keep them in constant dependance upon himself; God wisely carried them into a desolate wilderness: where they saw such continued, marvellous, instances of his power and goodness, as equally served to supply their continually-rising wants; and to strengthen and

I confirm

confirm their yet feeble, and wavering faith. For *there* their neceffities were not more various, urgent, and preffing; than his merciful providence was inftant, forward, and ready to relieve them: adapting itfelf to the circumftances of their condition, and adjufting its operations to the nature of their wants.

As they knew not the way through that pathlefs defart, and were in danger of being devoured by wild beafts; the *fhechinah*, the fymbol of the divine prefence, went conftantly before them, to guide and protect them in all their journies. " He fpread out a cloud for a covering in the day-time; and fire to give light in the night-feafon [x]."

When they grew thirfty, and had nothing to drink; " he brought waters out of the ftony rock, and gave them drink thereof as if it had been out of the great depth [y]."

When they were oppreffed with hunger, and had nothing to eat; " he fent them

[x] Pf. cv. 39.
[y] Pf. lxxviii. 15, 16. Ex. xvii. 6. Numb. xx. 8—11.

flefh

flefh in abundance, and filled them with the bread of heaven[z]."

As they were continually expofed to the inclemencies of the weather, without any means of fupplying themfelves with new cloathing; therefore, that they might not perifh by cold and nakednefs, he preferved their garments frefh and entire, through all the time of their migration in the wildernefs[a].

And, laftly, to render them equal to the difficulties of their marches, he kept their feet from fwelling, and their fhoes from wearing out[b].

The paternal care, difplayed in thefe miracles, muft, one would imagine, effectually engage their gratitude to God, " who had done fuch great things for them ;" and invariably fix them in a dutiful obedience to all his laws : laws, that were, moft of them, attended at their delivery with an amazing.

[z] Pf. cv. 40. Ex. xvi. 12—15. Numb. xi. 7, 31.
[a] Deut. xxix. 5.
[b] Deut. viii. 4.

2   train

train of wonders—equally calculated to prove their divinity, as to fecure them refpect and attention : laws, that were, all of them, excellently adapted, as well to promote the great defign of this people's feparation, as to prevent the irregularities, which they were liable to fall into, from the feducing examples of other nations.

But alas! fo ftrangely was this perverfe generation attached to the cuftoms, follies and fuperftitions of the people they had left, that no miracles could engage them, no laws could preferve them, in the allegiance they owed to God. For, even in defiance of the Ten Commandments which were juft delivered ; and while Sinai was yet trembling at the majeftic and awful prefence of the Almighty ; this people had the hardinefs to revolt from him—to make for themfelves a molten image—a golden calf, the very Egyptian Apis ᶜ—under the conduct and protec-

---

ᶜ Ὁ μόσχος ᾧτος, ὁ Ἄπις καλεύμενος. HERODOT. lib. iii. c. 28. Vide et SUIDAM in voce Ἄπιδις; which affords an excellent Comment on Exod. xxxii. 1—10.

tion

tion of which they meant to return to their beloved Egypt.

This defection was foul and daring: and as it deserved, so it accordingly received, a just and suitable punishment. " For there fell of the people that day about three thou-sand men[d]." But, notwithstanding this and other chastisements, which plainly shewed them the extreme folly of deserting their God; yet could not their hearts be in any wise induced to rely wholly upon him; nor could any motives prevail with them to " continue stedfast in his covenant[e]." They revolted from him at every turn; and mur-mured against him in every distress: which only served to increase their calamities, as it provoked his farther resentment.

When they perceived at length, that their rebellions against him served only to multiply the proofs of his supremacy, and to bring upon themselves heavier inflictions; their perverseness took then another turn;

[d] Ex. xxxii. 28.
[e] Psal. lxxviii. 37.

and

and vented itſelf in oppoſition to his *miniſters*. They diſputed both the title of Moſes to the *civil* power, and the deſignation of Aaron to the *prieſthood*[f].

Now this oppoſition was no leſs impious than arrogant. For it ſtruck directly at the very baſis of the divine eſtabliſhment; and was, in effect, an open declaration, that the Moſaic œconomy was nothing more, than a refined ſtroke of ſtate policy—the artful contrivance of their ambitious leader.

At the head of this oppoſition appeared two renowned and powerful parties; who, reſpectively, objected to the two brothers, Moſes and Aaron, on account of the offices, which they had reſpectively aſſumed. For Dathan and Abiram, who were the deſcendants of Reuben, the firſt-born of Jacob, thought themſelves, in right of primogeniture, better entitled to the *civil* authority, than Moſes could poſſibly be. And Korah and his adherents, being all, probably, of the tribe of Levi, claimed, in conſequence,

[f] Numb. xvi. 3.

an

an equal right with Aaron and his fons to the office of the *priefthood.*

Thefe were points of high concern; and required a clear, inconteftable decifion. But who could decide them, fave God himfelf? To him therefore the appeal was made. " And Mofes faid to all the affembly— Hereby ye fhall know, that the Lord hath fent me to do all thefe things ; and that I have not done them of mine own mind. If thefe men," who queftion my commiffion, " die the common death of all men; or if they be vifited after the vifitation of all men; then the Lord hath not fent me: but if the Lord make a new thing," and perform an inftant, tremendous miracle ; " if the earth open her mouth, and fwallow them up alive; then ye fhall underftand, that thefe men have provoked the Lord₅," in doubting my authority.

" And it came to pafs, fays the text, that, as he had made an end of fpeaking thefe words, the ground clave afunder that was

₅ Numb. xvi. 28—30.

under

under them; and the earth opened her mouth, and fwallowed them up, with all that appertained to them;—and then elofed again upon them [h]." A judgement, as decifive, as it was terrible.

Mofes's commiffion being thus proved, his brother's caufe was foon after determined. The trial was fair and open. Both parties appeared before the Lord, exercifing the duty of the office they claimed. But the great Judge of both inftantly declared his utter abhorrence of Korah's prefumption, by deftroying him and his affociates with fire [i]. And the next day he publicly ratified his approbation of Aaron, by accepting the atonement he made for the people, and ftopping the plague that was raging among them [k].

When God, by thefe tremendous acts, had clearly manifefted his choice of Aaron, in preference to the fons of Levi; he was

[b] Numb. xvi. 31—33.
[i] Ib. ver. 35.
[k] Ib. ver. 48.

afterwards

afterwards pleafed, in order to prevent any farther conteft, to confirm the fame by another miracle, to the exclufion of *all* the tribes. The form of the procedure was this; and is ftriking. He ordered them to take twelve *almond-rods*[1], according to the number of the twelve tribes; upon one of which the chief perfon of every tribe was to infcribe his name; and the name of Aaron to be written on the rod of Levi.

Now, if we fuppofe, as I think we may, that the *almond tree* was ufed in ancient times for the emblem of favour, acceptance and propitioufnefs[m]; then it will appear, that, by this defignation, each rod became

---

[1] Numb. xvii. 1—5.

[m] Servius, in his comment on the following lines of Virgil, Georg. i. 187, &c.

Contemplator item, cum fe nux plurima fyl.is,

Induit in forem, et ramos curvabit olentes;

Si fuperant fœtus, pariter frumenta fequentur, &c.

obferves, Prognofticon eft anni futuri fertilis, cum multis amygdala vefliet fe floribus, &c. " that the quick budding, bloffoming, &c. of the *almond* tree, were looked upon as a fure fign of a kind, plentiful and propitious year." And therefore might eafily be transferred to reprefent *favour*, *profperity*, or *propitioufnefs* at large.

not

not only the fymbol of a particular tribe,
but alfo the emblem of the *priefily* office, in
its higheft and moft important branch, the
article of *atonement.* And if fo, we have a
clear view at once, as well of the propriety
of this mode of proceeding ; as of the juft-
nefs of the conclufion, which immediately
refulted from it. For if thefe rods, depofited
in the tabernacle, remained there all together (that of Aaron alone excepted) in a *dry,*
dead and *lifelefs* ftate ; was it not evident
even to a demonftration, that the tribes reprefented by them were to remain *powerlefs*
and *without authority,* in regard to the offices
of that holy place ? And when " the rod of
Aaron *budded, bloffomed,* and yielded *fruit,*"
in fo wonderful a manner, how plainly,
though fymbolically, it was thereby determined, that he and his defcendants were
the only perfons, whom the Lord had
called to minifter before him ; and that
their miniftration alone was the miniftration of *truth, life* and *perfeÉtion ?* And as *this*
rod was afterwards laid up in the ark, for a
perpetual teftimony of the divine eleÉtion of
the

the *Aaronic* race[n]; fo were " the *cenfers* of Korah and his company wrought out into broad plates for a covering of the altar, as a ftanding memorial of the dreadful effect of their impious rebellion—that none, for the future, might prefume to rebel in the fame manner[o]."

And indeed, rebellions of this kind they were no longer guilty of; though in other refpects they continued ftill incorrigibly vile, perverfe and difobedient.

For, when God had carried them, with much patience and long-fuffering, to the very borders of the promifed land ; and had mercifully propofed to put an end to their travels; forgetful of his mighty works, and actuated again by a fpirit of perverfenefs, they contemptuoufly defpifed that pleafant land ; and, concluding him unable to give them poffeffion of it, murmured againft him

[n] Numb. xvii. 10.

[o] Numb. xvi. 38--40. When king Uzziah, many years after, impioufly tranfgreffed in the fame way, he was inftantly and miraculoufly fmitten with the leprofy, and continued infected to the day of his death. 2 Chron. xxvi. 16---21.

with

with great bitternefs, for expofing them to
the dangers and calamities of war. "Where-
fore hath the Lord brought us unto this
land, to fall by the fword; that our wives
and our children fhould be made a prey?
Were it not better for us, to chufe a captain,
and return again into Egypt?" And a
captain they accordingly chofe q.

This audacious revolt, proceeding from a
fpirit of hardened infidelity, provoked the
Almighty to fuch a degree, that he determined to reject that whole generation, and
force them to wander about in the wildernefs, till they were all confumed and worn
away. How they fpent their time there,
the prophets will readily inform us. "Have
ye offered unto me," faith God by the mouth
of Amos, " facrifices and offerings in the
wildernefs by the fpace of forty years, O
houfe of Ifrael r?" No: but, as he farther
complains in the words of Ezekiel, " The
houfe of Ifrael rebelled againft me in the

p Numb. xiv. 3, 4.
q Nehem. ix. 17.
r Ch. v. 25.

wildernefs:

wilderneſs : they walked not in my ſtatutes;
and they deſpiſed my judgements; and my
ſabbaths they greatly polluted; and their
heart went after their idols ˢ." And ſince
they choſe for themſelves theſe vain gods,
therefore the Lord " conſumed their days in
correſpondent vanity, and the years they had
to live in extreme trouble ᵗ."

When this faithleſs generation was thus
condemned to wander about, and die away,
by degrees, in the wilderneſs; the Lord, to
give fuller ſcope to the ſentence, withdrew
from them, in ſome meaſure, that gracious
protection which he had before vouchſafed;
and ſuffered them to periſh, partly by the
natural annoyances of the country; ſuch as
the bite of venemous ſerpents ᵘ, and other
calamities incident to travellers in hot cli-
mates; and partly by the incurſions of ad-
jacent enemies ˣ; who eaſily overcame them,
when now their God no longer ſuccoured
them.

ˢ Ch. xx. 13, 16.
ᵗ Pſal. lxxviii. 33.
ᵘ Numb. xxi. 6.
ˣ Ibid. xiv. 45.

In

In this natural and ordinary way, which sufficiently anfwered the purpofe of Provi-dence, were numbers of them carried off—to the great abatement of ill examples. But whenever they " finned with an high hand," and were guilty of prefumptuous tranfgref-fions; then did they always feel and expe-rience the immediate rigour of divine ven-geance, in a fearful and extraordinary man-ner. They were confumed by fire, or fwept away by a plague. Of thefe inflictions we have feveral inftances: but none more re-markable, than that which happened " in the matter of Peor;" when, for their heinous and complicated offence—their bafe idolatry and fhamelefs fornication—" there fell of them in one day four and twenty thou-fand [y]." This was the laft and finifhing ftroke of God's avenging providence; which, to the happy deliverance of the fucceeding race, completed the excifion of that corrupt generation.

In the mean time however; whilft he ex-ercifed thefe marvellous, unrelenting feveri-

[y] Numb. xxv. 9. 1 Cor. x. 8.

ties

ties againſt that ſtubborn and devoted generation; it is no leſs curious than pleaſing to
obſerve, with what infinite condeſcenſion, as
well as kindneſs, he undertook the guardian-
ſhip of their riſing progeny; with what af-
fectionate care he watched and defended the
infirmities of their youth; and with what
unwearied diligence he formed their minds,
and regulated their manners, as they grew
up.   To this end, he renewed his covenant
with them: he repeatedly inſtructed them in
all the momentous parts of his law: he laid
before them various motives to engage them
in the faithful obſervance of it: and " he led
them about" with their devoted fathers;
that, ſeeing in their puniſhment the miſera-
ble conſequences of apoſtaſy and diſobedience, they might cautiouſly avoid ſuch pernicious examples, as would prompt them to
neglect or tranſgreſs their duty.

Theſe were excellent means of improvement.   And as by theſe means they were
trained up into a right notion of the divine
majeſty; and early impreſſed with a deep
ſenſe of his ſupreme authority; ſo by the

continued

continued application of ftrict difcipline, and
the conftant difplay of miraculous power,
they were brought at length to be tolerably
well attached to his government, and eftablifhed in his pure worfhip.

When they became thus tractable, dutiful and obedient; and had approved themfelves as fit agents for carrying on the purpofes of his providence; God then conducted them towards the land of Canaan—
the place of their deftined habitation; and
affured them, if they continued faithful, of
their fpeedy conqueft and poffeffion of it.

And, here, to engage their reliance upon
him, and to ftrengthen their confidence the
more in him, he recounted to them his
former promifes; and appealed to their own
experience how punctual he had been in the
accomplifhment of them. He put them in
mind, that, though he had been obliged to
chaftize them for their benefit, and even to
cut off from among them the refractory and
infectious; he had neverthelefs been ftill
true and faithful to his word; ftill careful
of the main body; fince it appeared by the

muſter now taken, that their number on the whole was nearly as great, if not greater than it was before[z]. And if, in a ſtate of diſobedience, they were not diminiſhed by the hand of God; they might well conclude, that, in the proſecution of their duty, they ſhould never be deſtroyed by the hands of men.

But, notwithſtanding the concluſion they might draw from hence; as the undertaking they were ſoon to enter upon was ſeemingly difficult and full of danger, ſo God was pleaſed to afford them ſtill more obvious proofs, and to ſupport them by ſtill more animating encouragements. He led them on againſt ſeveral powerful, idolatrous nations; who oppoſed and obſtructed their paſſage: and over theſe he vouchſafed them an eaſy conqueſt, as a pledge of their future ſucceſs in Canaàn. For they muſt needs look upon what he had now done, as an earneſt of what he had promiſed to do farther, for them.

[z] Comp. Numb. xxvi. 51, 62. with Exod. xxxviii. 26.

Such

Such then was the progrefs of divine adminiftration, during the abode of the Ifraelites
in the wildernefs. And from the whole tenour of this adminiftration it appears; that
the great point, which God had more immediately in view, was to fit and difpofe this
wavering people to anfwer the end for
which they were chofen: that his chief
point was, to " humble them, and to prove
them—" to bring them clofe, and attach
them, to himfelf; that, being at length
firmly bound to his fervice, they might be
ready and willing, as it was defigned they
fhould, to promote his true religion and
worfhip, in oppofition to the reigning idolatry.

And upon this foundation it is eafy to account for all the ftatutes and judgements he
gave them; and for all the preffing exhortations to the careful obfervance of thofe ftatutes and laws[a]. It is eafy to account for
the eminent bleffings annexed to obedience;
and for the curfes denounced againft vice,

[a] Deut. iv. 1—40.

and

and apoftacy [b]. It is eafy to account for the
ftrict prohibition of all communication with
the idolatrous nations [c]; for the feeming feverity of commanding their cities to be all
deftroyed, together with the monuments of
their fuperftitious worfhip [d]; and alfo, for
the abolition of all cuftoms, which had any
reference to fuch practices [e]. The neceffities
of the times, the welfare of religion, and the
improvement of the world, called for thefe
things.   For they were all, either fo many
motives to, and enforcements of, true piety;
or prudent cautions, and needful barriers,
againft the encroachments of wickednefs and
idolatry.

Thus then we fee what proper provifion
was continually made for the knowledge and
adoration of the true God, among his peculiar and chofen people; and how well they
became qualified thereby to advance the defign and purpofe of his providence, with re-

[b] Deut. xxviii. 1—68.
[c] Ibid. vii. 1---5.
[d] Ibid. xii. 1—3.
[e] Ibid. xiv. 1. 3.—xvi. 21, 22.

gard

gard to the reft of the world. And knowing now that it was in his purpofe from the
beginning, to make " all the nations of the
earth finally bleffed" through this difpenfation; what thanks fhould we render to the
Lord for his goodnefs; who, notwithftanding the favours he fhewed to the Ifraelites,
" had ftill provided fome better and nobler
thing for us that they, without us, might
not be made perfect ᶠ."

Now to God the Father, Son, and Holy
Ghoft, be afcribed, as is moft due, all honour and glory, world without end. *Amen.*

ᶠ Heb. xi. 40.

T 3   S E R-

SERMON XII.

PSAL. xliv. ver. 3.

For they got not the land in poſſeſſion by their
own ſword, neither did their own arm ſave
them: but thy right hand, and thine arm, and
the light of thy countenance; becauſe thou
hadſt a favour unto them.

WHEN the Almighty had raiſed up,
in the manner related, proper inhabitants for the land of Canaan, his miraculous providence conducted them to it, and
gave them poſſeſſion of it.

Now, as the conqueſt of this land was
firſt promiſed, and then ſecured to them,

T 4

not

not merely for their own fake, but rather as
a means of carrying on the grand defign,
which God had originally purpofed; fo it is
natural to prefume, that the meafures, by
which it was to be now achieved, muft bear
fome reference to that defign, and contribute in their degree to the promotion of it.
And indeed, if we fedately confider thefe
meafures, and clofely obferve their effects
and tendencies, we fhall find them adapted,
with exquifite propriety, to the advancement
of the end in view;—to the extirpation of
idolatry, and the eftablifhment of true religion. For they all confpired to fill the nations with wonder and aftonifhment; to im-
print on their minds high conceptions of the
majefty of Jehovah; and to render them
fenfible of the fin and folly of placing their
reliance, hope or confidence in any other
God but him.

To evince the truth of this affertion, let
us firft attend to the general plan, that was
laid down for the acquifition of the country.
It was to be undertaken and profecuted by
war. Now, had the acquifition of the
country

country been the whole that was intended, it is eafy to conceive, that God might have accomplifhed it in a different manner from that which depended on the force of arms. He might have deftroyed the inhabitants by famine or peftilence; and introduced his people into all their poffeffions without the trouble of drawing a fword. But this mode of proceeding, however effectual in gaining the land, would feemingly have anfwered no higher purpofes. It would neither have ma-nifefted to the world the power and great-nefs of the *true* God, nor expofed to view the weaknefs and futility of *falfe* deities: whereas the *other* method brought thefe points directly to the teft, and made them obvious to all people. For all nations hav-ing then their tutelary deities, to whofe pro-tection they committed themfelves and their country; and of whofe power they judged by the fate of war; it is evident, that an at-tack upon any country was virtually an at-tack on thofe guardian gods, who were fup-pofed to be the defenders of it; and whofe ftrength was put to a trial in the conteft.

Hence

Hence then it follows, that this war in Canaan was a kind of *holy war*; maintained on the one side by the worſhipers of Jehovah in oppoſition to the idolatrous nations on the other. The ſuccefs therefore, which he vouchſafed his people, muſt be acknowledged, even on the principles of heathenifm, to have been a full proof of his ſuperior power, and ſovereign authority over their idol gods: and conſequently muſt be looked upon as an excellent mean to convince them of the abſurdity of depending on ſuch gods, in preference to the God of Iſrael: as it muſt alſo be a ſtrong and forcible motive to induce them now to alter their opinion; and to adopt him for the object of their worſhip, who was *poſſeſſed*, and ſhewed them he *was* poſſeſſed, of ſo great and uncontroulable a power.

And that his power might appear ſtill more conſpicuous, ſtill more inconteſtable; he diſpoſed, we are to obſerve, the whole train of operations in ſuch a manner, that the conqueſt was made not only with eaſe and rapidity; but alſo made by a young, raw,

unpractiſed

unpractifed infantry, fighting, at all difad-
vantages, with ftrong, hardy, experienced
veterans, fupported by a numerous cavalry.
A circumftance which clearly demonftrated,
that " they gat not the land in poffeffion
through their own fword;" but by the marvellous affiftance of his arm, who, " at the
inftant he fpeaketh concerning a nation or
kingdom, to build and to plant it, or to pull
down and deftroy it [g]," can accordingly bring
it to pafs.

But let us now quit thefe *general* reflections; and proceed to inveftigate thofe
fpecial inferences, which may be farther
drawn, to the fame purpofe, from the confideration of the *particular* achievements
recorded.

It has been already obferved, that the
war now waged in the land of Canaan may
properly be called *the war of the Lord*; as
being carried on with a view of planting in
that land his true religion and pure worfhip,
inftead of thofe deteftable rites of idolatry,
that were then univerfally practifed. Agree-

[g] Jer. xviii. 7, 9.

ably

ably therefore to fuch an intention, God, at this time, joined the religious to the regal character; and preceded his people, not merely as the governor or king of Ifrael, but exprefly as " the Lord of the whole earth[h];" as that fovereign Being, who had a juft right to the homage and obedience of all mankind; and might equitably punifh their contempt or refufal.

To make them fenfible, that he came now to demand his right, and to eftablifh his worfhip among them; he ordered the ark (the fymbol of his *prefence*, and the facred repofitory of his *law*) to be taken up by the priefts, the minifters of his religion; and to be conducted forwards to that land, where he had promifed, and was determined, to fix it. And that nothing might be wanting to influence and perfwade the inhabitants of the land to give it proper reception; and to accept the Lord, whofe ark it was, for the object of their faith and worfhip; he plainly fhewed them, that his prefence was continually with it—and that his power was en-

[h] Jofh. iii. 13.

gaged

gaged to fupport thofe in every emergency, who attended it, revered it, and were attached to it. For no fooner " were the feet of the priefts dipped in the brim of the water," but the overflowing of Jordan inftantly retired; fo that its channel became, and continued, dry, " until all the people were paffed over[i]."

This miracle, one would judge, might be fufficient in reafon to awaken the Canaanites to a due fenfe of the majefty of Jehovah; and, confequently, to a due acknowledgement of the right he claimed to their fubmiffion, their worfhip, and their obedience. But the men of Jericho, blindly devoted to their own deities, overlooked the grandeur of this mighty act, and, contemptuoufly refufing the overtures that were made, prepared themfelves to oppofe his people.

Provoking as this conduct really was, yet God, patient and long-fuffering, unwilling that they fhould perifh, and folicitous that

[i] Jofh. iii. 15---17. The paffage now opened for the Ifraelites was about eighteen miles in breadth; and therefore the more wonderful.

they

they might repent, gracioufly allowed them
time to reflect; and prefled them to comply by repeated applications for the fpace of
feven days together.   All this, though it has
lain unnoticed, is manifeftly implied in the
account we have of the proceedings at the
fiege of Jericho.

When the Ifraelites, by the command of
God, marched round the city in the order
defcribed [k]; it is natural to conclude, from
the wifdom of him who gave the command, that it was done with fome great and
inftructive defign; with a view to convey
fome falutary leffon.   To our commentators
indeed this tranfaction has unhappily appeared in no higher light, than that of fhew
or paftime; and has been treated by unbelievers accordingly.   But to the befieged, I
am convinced, it appeared in a different, and
a very important, light.   For they muft
needs know, if they knew any thing of the
modes of the times, and the cuftoms of
their own country, that the whole was a

k Jofh. vi. 3---16.

folemn,

folemn, religious proceffion[1]. They muft
needs know, if they knew the rites of their
own worfhip, that " the priefts blowing
with the trumpets" was a loud call or invitation to them to come out and join the ark;
and to adore the God to whom it belonged.
And they muft needs alfo know, if they
knew the grounds of their own military ex-
hibitions, that " the armed men walking
before," was a pofitive, though emblematical, declaration—that, in cafe they perfifted
to flight and rejeĉt thefe gracious invitations;
thefe overtures of mercy now made; the
fword would overtake them with relentlefs

---

[1] VIRGIL, who is peculiarly accurate in his accounts of ancient manners, reprefents Dido, a Tyrian, and confequently a
defcendant of this very people, as making a *folemn, religious pro-*
ceffion exaĉtly in the fame form: Æneid. IV. ver. 63.

Aut ante ora Deûm pingues fpatiatur ad aras.

" She walks *before* the images of her gods quite *round* the altar."
And that the Jews obferved the fame cuftom, is evident from the
Pfalmift's allufion—" And fo will I *compafs* thine altar." Pfal.
xxvi. 6. See alfo Nehem. xii. 27---43. And Jericho may not
improperly be confidered now as an altar; whereon " the Lord,"
to fpeak in the words of the prophet Jeremiah, xlvi. 10. " had
great facrifice to make."

fury,

fury, and punifh their obftinacy by a total excifion [m].

Now, knowing this to be the true language, and real meaning of the prefent tranfaction; how juftly did they deferve to fall under the vengeance of that God, whofe power and goodnefs they had fo perverfely defpifed! And how demonftrably evident was

[m] To explain the intention, and illuftrate the meaning of this complex ceremony, it may be proper to obferve, 1. that *trumpets* were ufed among all people for two different purpofes: to *call affemblies*, when they blew a *clear, fhort* blaft; and to found an *alarm* for the onfet of battle, when they made a *rough* and *long* blaft. Now, here they are employed in both thefe ways—in the way of *call* or *invitation* by *fhort* blafts, during the feveral proceffions; and, at laft, in the way of *alarm* by a *long* blaft, (comp. ver. 5. and 10.) when the city was to be affaulted. Hence then it appears, that the city was not attacked, till the inhabitants had *thirteen* feveral times rejected the overtures, that were made to them; and this, even when they underftood, that the Ifraelites were determined to punifh their refufal. For it is to be obferved, 2. that the *armed men* going before, were, in a military view, juft fo many *heralds at arms*; who, by their movements and geftures, fignificantly declared to the inhabitants of Jericho, that, if they obftinately perfifted to reject their offers, efpecially when urged in a folemn manner for *feven* days together, (the utmoft term allowed for deliberation; fee 1 Sam. xi. 3.) they muft expect to feel the rigour of their vengeance in a fearful and total deftruction.

it,

it, that the Ifraelites were charged with his
fpecial commiffion, when " the wall of the
city fell down flat," or rather; " funk quite
level with the ground[n]," to fmooth their
paffage for the deftruction of that people;
which had impioufly " defied the armies of
the living God?" And if this amazing overthrow was completed on the *fabbath*; on the
day peculiarly devoted to the honour and
fervice of the God of Ifrael[o]; how plainly
muft it appear to be the judgement of his
hand for the contempt thrown on his religious character? And upon the whole, what
a fignificant prognoftic, what a fure earneft
was there given hereby to the whole world,
that his religion and worfhip, however defpifed, would finally prevail over all the oppofition that could ever be made to its
growth and eftablifhment?

Now, if the vengeance taken, in fo marvellous a manner, on this obftinate and im-

[n] Jofh. vi. 20.

[o] Vide Talmud Babylonic. Tract. de Sabbatho cap. I. RAY-
MUND. MARTINI Pug. Fidei, cum obferv. Jos. DE VOISIN.
p. iii. dift. iii. cap. xi. § 29. p. 625.

pious city, could have no influence on the reft of the nations, to make them renounce their wickednefs and idolatry, and furrender themfelves to God and his people; what elfe can in juftice be expected to follow, but that, fince they chofe to perfift in the fame crime, they fhould feel the rigour of the fame punifhment? They had warning fufficient given them. And what they faw executed with fo much feverity, fhould have induced them to avoid what was farther threatned. The fall of Jericho, and the deftruction of Ai, at the fame time that they were punifhments to fome, were admonitions to others. And how well they were adapted to work on ferious and confiderate minds, is evident from the conduct of the Gibeonites; who, though they had probably difregarded the propofals, which the Ifraelites had made, at firft [p], were yet now perfectly convinced,

that

---

[p] That the Ifraelites made offers of peace to the Canaanites, on condition they renounced their falfe deities, and acknowledged Jehovah for their only God; is evident, I think, from what has been faid in explaining the fiege of Jericho. But the fame may be ftill more clearly deduced from the precept deli-

vered

that it was madnefs and folly to continue the oppofition; and hence prudently became dif- pofed, not only to forfake their idol gods, but to feek the friendfhip of the children of Ifrael; to join them in the worfhip and fer- vice of the Lord—in the belief and practice of true religion.

Such prudence, however, was the happy lot of thefe men alone. The other ftates re-

vered in Deut. xx. 10, &c. where it appears, that propofals of peace were to be made to all nations: but peace being refufed, they were to proceed in a more rigorous manner with the Ca- naanites, than with any *other* people: of the latter, to kill only the *males*; of the former, to fave *nothing* alive that breathed. Some writers, indeed, have been led to conclude, from what we read in the 15th verfe, that this privilege belonged only " to thofe cities, which were not of the cities of the Canaanites." But this is a wrong conclufion: and muft needs appear wrong to any one, who attentively confiders the reflection that occurs Jofh. xi. 19, 20. " There was no city that made peace with the children of Ifrael, fave the Hivites, the inhabitants of Gibeon; all other they took in battle. For it was of the Lord to harden their hearts, that they fhould come againft Ifrael to battle, that he might deftroy them utterly, and *that they might have no fa- vour*—" which manifeftly implies, that if they had fought peace, and not come out to battle, they might have obtained *favour*, and not been deftroyed. That the Jews underftood the text in this fenfe, is evident from Menasseh Ben Israel's Conciliator, Quæft. viii. in Deut. p. 230, &c.

U 2   mained

mained ftill under the wretched influence of blind zeal, and infatuated fuperftition. Actuated then by a ftrongly envenomed and fuperftitious fpirit, the five kings of the Amorites immediately combined together, and determined to extirpate the inhabitants of Gibeon, as traytors to their country, and apoftates from its guardian gods. Hereupon therefore the Lord, whofe honour was concerned in the fupport of his new converts, commanded Jofhua to fuccour the Gibeonites; and, by way of encouragement, affured him of a complete and decifive victory over that powerful army, which had injurioufly affaulted this innocent people. Jofhua, in obedience to the divine command, " fell fuddenly on the Amorites; " flew them with a great flaughter ꝗ;" and put them to a total rout. But then, left the victory fhould be attributed to the fole prowefs and management of the Ifraelittes, the Lord, 'tis to be obferved, fo conducted the order of the battle, that his power was feen in feveral

ꝗ Jofh. x. 9, 10.

incidents;

incidents; and his superiority over the heathen deities displayed to the view of all. For
the three principal deities, whom the Amorites adored, and in vindication of whose
violated honour they seem to have entered
on the present attempt, were the Sun, Moon,
and Heavens or Air. To convince them
therefore that these gods were entirely subject to the God of Israel; and to punish
them, at the same time, for the false worship
they paid them; "the Lord thundered
against them from heaven, and showered
in their faces great hailstones ͬ from the air,
which flew vast numbers of them·;" and
then stopt the two great *luminaries* in their
course, till the Israelites had completely
vanquished the remainder ͭ." And God, it
should seem, inspired now the Hebrew general to call for this miracle " in the sight
of Israel," to deter them from the practice

ͬ Or perhaps *real stones*, many showers of which history records to have happened. See CALMET's Dissertation on the
subject.

ˢ Josh. x. ver. 11.

ͭ Ibid. ver. 12.

of

of the like idolatry; " from kiffing their hands," as the manner was, " when they beheld the fun as it fhined, or the moon walking in brightnefs [u]."

It may be thought perhaps, that the only motive, which induced Jofhua to put up his prayer for the prolongation of the day, was his earneft defire of gaining time to purfue his advantages; which otherwife, he apprehended, would be too fhort for the entire conqueft and fubverfion of his enemies. But this, if indeed any motive at all, appears, however, from the circumftances of the narration, to be neither the only one, nor the chief. The mere finifhing fuch a conqueft feems to be fcarce a fufficient ground for fo extraordinary a petition. But admit it was; yet, how came the petition to be offered up at fuch a time? When the requeft was made, the greateft part of the enemy was deftroyed, and the reft put to the rout: the day was but half fpent, and the fun in the

[u] Job xxxi. 26. 27.

meri-

meridian ^x. Now, what is there to be difcovered in the prefent circumftances, that
could prompt the victorious and triumphant
general to require fuch a miracle to be
wrought in his behalf? He had light fufficient before him, in all probability, to accomplifh his defigns: or, if he found the
victory unexpectedly retarded, would it not
have been time enough to petition for a
longer day, when he faw the fun low in its
declenfion, and near its fetting? Thefe confiderations would lead one to conclude that
the prayer, now preferred by Jofhua, was
rather the effect of a divine impulfe, than the
refult of his reflections on the event of the
day; and that the chief purport of the miracle, exhibited in anfwer to it, was to convince both armies, and all who obferved it,
" that the gods of the heathens were but
idols; and that it was the Lord who made,

---

x For the *Heb.* text fays—" So the fun ftood ftill בחצי
השמים in the *midft of heaven,* or in the *mid-heaven*; and hafted
not to *go down* or *decline* about a whole day." ver. 13.

—Κατὰ ΜΕΣΟΝ τῦ ὑρανῦ᾽ ὀ προεπορεύετο εἰς δυσμάς. LXX.

— In *medio* cœli, neque feftinavit ad occafum. *Syr.*

U 4   and

and who governed the heavens^y." This at
least muft be acknowledged; that it was admirably adapted to work fuch a conviction,
whatever ends it might ferve befides.

Marvellous and furprifing as Jofhua's conqueft of thefe *fouthern* provinces appears; yet
fo blind, and fo inconfiderate were the *nor-*
thern kings, that they neither recognized
therein the power of the Lord, nor indeed
perceived " the operation of his hands." On
the contrary, they attributed the misfortune,
which their brethren fuftained, to their fighting in fmall parties; to their bringing erro-
neoufly into the field an inadequate number
of men; and trufting folely to the valour
of their *infantry*. In remedy therefore of
fo fatal an errour, thefe kings warily united
their forces; " and went out, they and all
their hofts with them; much people, even
as the fand that is upon the fea-fhore in multitude, with *horfes* and *chariots* very many:
and they pitched together at the waters of
Merom, to fight againft Ifrael^z." This army

y Pfal. xcvi. 5.
z Jofh. xi. 4, 5.

5

was

was truly formidable; confifting, if we may believe Jofephus, of no lefs than " three hundred thoufand footmen, fupported by ten thoufand *horfemen,* and twenty thoufand *chariots* [a]." But, numerous and formidable as they were, God commanded his people to attack them; and upon this attack—to fhew them that " he was the God of forces;" to manifeft to the world, that " no king can be faved by the multitude of an hoft;" and that horfes and chariots were but vain inftruments of defence againft his avenging power: to make *them,* I fay, and *others* through them, duly fenfible of thefe things; he " delivered them up into the hand of Ifrael; who chafed and fmote them till they were all deftroyed[b];" and who then got fpeedy pofleffion of their country—divided it among themfelves—and enjoyed it without farther difturbance.

Thus have we feen by what means Canaan was conquered; and in what manner its wicked and idolatrous inhabitants were deftroyed. If we review thefe means by the

[a] JOSEPH. Ant. Jud. lib. v. c. i. § 18.
[b] Jofh. xi. 8.

light

light which has now been thrown upon
them; we fhall find them in their nature
wifely appropriated, and in their effects har-
monioufly confpiring, to that firft and great
defign, which Providence had conftantly in
view;—the confutation and abolition of idolatry. And if we confider what an evil idolatry was; how exceffively it weakened all
the principles of religion and virtue; and
how amazingly it encouraged all manner of
vice and wickednefs; we fhall find it to be
a defign, truly worthy both of the wifdom
and goodnefs of God, to put a ftop to its
fpreading contagion. And if it fhould appear to be fo widely fpread and firmly rooted,
that its growth and progrefs could not be
ftopped, but by the extirpation of thofe, who
were moft infamous for the practice of it;
then furely fuch an act of excifion, when the
people were paft all hopes of amendment,
would be fo far from being an act of cruelty
or injuftice, that it would perfectly accord
with all the rules of the ftricteft equity: and
however fevere it might feem to the fuffer-
ers, muft be an act of mercy to the reft of
the

SERMON XII. 299

the world.—Now such, in fact, was the
case before us.

The Canaanites were a people deeply im-
mersed in the superstitions of idolatry ; and,
as the natural consequence of it, in the
shameful practice of the most abominable
impurities, of the most flagitious crimes, and
the most inhuman cruelties [c]. Various means
had been already employed to correct and reform their manners. Could milder methods
have prevailed, the examples and conversa-
tion of the holy patriarchs would have won
and engaged them. Had harsher measures
been of any effect, the tremendous destruction
of Sodom and Gomorrah would have awed
and alarmed them. Or had the present ma-
nifestations been of any avail, the gracious
overtures made to all would have either
allured them ; or, the consequent punish-
ments inflicted on some, would have moved
others to better obedience. But their perverseness was incorrigible. They would still
maintain their idolatrous principles—still per-
severe in their vicious practices.

[c] Wisd. xii. 3—6, 11.

In

In compaffion therefore to the world, and for the benefit of the reft of mankind, as thefe people could not be reclaimed, God determined to cut them off. And fince their iniquities called for fuch an exemplary punifhment; how wifely was it ordained, that it fhould be executed upon them by the hand of Ifrael, in preference to any other method [d]! In this form it carried with it a public condemnation of that idolatry, to which their vices were chiefly owing; and ferved to deftroy the root of thefe evils, as well as to demonftrate the indignation of God againft thofe who were guilty of them. Nor could thefe ends have been fo fully anfwered in any other manner. Unfruitful and unhealthy feafons might eafily have been interpreted ufual and common accidents. Plagues, fire from heaven, peftilences or famine might be thought to proceed from the difpleafure of their own deities; and to be capable of being either prevented or removed by certain fuper-

---

[d] JENKIN's Reafon. of the Chr. Rel. vol. I. p. 72. LOWMAN's Differt. on the Civil Government of the Hebrews. ch. xii. p. 221, &c.

ftitious

ftitious or magical ceremonies. Such punifhments then, confidering the notions and difpofitions of the times, were extremely liable
to be mifconftrued; were likely to be abufed,
to add ftrength and vigour to idolatry, rather
than to weaken and root it out. But when
God made choice of a peculiar people, pro-
fefling his pure worfhip in plain oppofition to
all idolatry; when he granted this people the
poffeffion of Canaan, and enabled them by
his power to extirpate its wicked and fuperftitious inhabitants; this was fuch a triumph,
as clearly fhewed his abfolute dominion; and
conveyed to the world a vifible confutation
of the hope of idolaters: conveyed to the
world a manifeft proof, how vain it is to
truft or rely on any other God, but on Him
alone, " who is perfect in holinefs, as well
as mighty in works."

And as it ferved thus to bring over unbelievers to the acknowledgement and obedience of the one true God; fo did it contribute in an equal degree to keep his real
worfhipers on their guard; to make them
careful, that they might not be " drawn
by

by the errour of the wicked, to fall from
their own ftedfaftnefs[e]." For if the Canaanites were punifhed with fo much feverity for refufing to own Jehovah as God;
what muft the Ifraelites expect to fuffer, if
ever they became fo degenerate and bafe as
to fall away and apoftatize from him? Surely
they could not but be convinced, " that it
had been better" and more tolerable " for
them, not to have known the way of the
Lord, than, after they had known it, to
turn afide from the holy commandments delivered unto them[f]." And indeed, under
the force of this conviction, and in gratitude
for the kindnefs he had now fhewn them,
Ifrael, we are told, " ferved the Lord all the
days of Jofhua, and all the days of the el-
ders that out-lived Jofhua, and who had
known all the works of the Lord, which he
had done for Ifrael[g]."

Now to God the Father, &c. *Amen.*

[e] 2 Pet. iii. 7.
[f] 2 Pet. ii. 21.
[g] Judg. ii. 7.

E N D   O F   V O L.   I.

www.ingramcontent.com/pod-product-compliance
Lightning Source LLC
Chambersburg PA
CBHW021032030726
47496CB00006B/1504